Vintage CARAVAN Style

Vintage CARAVAN Style

BUYING, RESTORING, DECORATING AND STYLING
THE SMALL SPACES OF YOUR DREAMS

LISA MORA

D&C
David and Charles

Contents

CHAPTER 1

The joy of vintage caravans

A place to love

Once you've stepped inside one, it's hard not to fall in love with a vintage caravan or trailer. Moreover the chances are, if you don't already own one or more, you will probably wish you did. I remember that even as a youngster I fantasized about running away with a horse-drawn gypsy wagon, all brightly painted, to live my life on the road. It's somehow romantic, that dream of the wandering life in a caravan, free from obligations and commitments.

I think we all have moments when we long for a roaming lifestyle; it seems to be in our programming to experience wanderlust and feel the desire to roam from time to time. Home is a wonderful thing, but the appeal of life on the road is pretty exciting, too; the sensation that fills my heart when my trailer is all hooked up to the car and we are setting off on a road trip actually feels like my heart is unfurling wings and taking flight.

I love the excitement, the adventure of it all, the road and the scenery, but I also like the convenience of having my fully stocked wardrobe and bed all made up just as I like it and rolling along right behind me. Vintage trailers are cute, they are fun to decorate and they will happily road trip with you to any destination at a moment's notice – what's not to love about them?

(Right) This on-site 1960s Winnebago is available for hire at Enchanted Trails RV Park in Alberquerque, New Mexico, USA.

(Above) Love Vintage Caravans in New Zealand restored this gorgeous 1966 Silverstream 'Lola'.

(Above) Vintage trailerites from around the world love to collect any items that feature trailers.

A journey through time

Throughout history, caravanning as a form of travel has played a very significant part in our cultural development. Long before cars were invented, 'caravans' of camels travelling nose to tail were loaded with exotic goods and used by traders to travel long distances over vast deserts in search of new markets for their wares. In the Americas of the 1800s, covered wagons carried optimistic pioneer families and all their worldly possessions from one side of the country to another in search of a better life. Across Europe, the brightly painted horse-drawn wooden 'vardos' of the Romany gypsies allowed the travelling cultures to follow seasonal work.

The desire for greener pastures and better times ahead has been a motivator for the movement of people since time began; and no matter how sedentary our lifestyles have become, many of us still feel tugged by the allure of the road and an innate sense of adventure. Yet, as we have become more settled and domesticated, the allure of the road trip and holidays away from home have seen the caravan become more of a leisure vehicle rather than simply a convenient way to move things from one destination to another. As a result, from the 1940s onwards, camper trailers and purpose-built caravans began to sport awnings and annexes, ice boxes, gas cookers and lights, and the caravanning holiday started to become a popular way to enjoy quality time with friends and family.

(Far left) The glamorous world of caravanning as experienced in a 1940s Countess caravan.

(Left) The journeys of the early pioneers form a large part of the American psyche.

The allure of the open road is hard to resist.

The golden years

Up until the 1950s, many travel trailers and caravans had been homemade from plywood, using plans that could be purchased at hardware stores and in books. However, by the 1960s, cars started to sport larger, stronger and more reliable engines, and newer, more lightweight construction materials such as aluminium and fibreglass began to be incorporated into the construction of caravans and travel trailers.

This meant that commercially produced caravans built during this golden era of caravanning between the 1960s and 1970s were lighter, stronger, easier to tow and more affordable than ever before. Caravanning and camping holidays became treasured times during which fond family memories were created; they also became a popular choice for honeymooning couples to spend some time sharing a space and getting to know one another before they moved into their own home.

As their original owners aged, many of the caravans produced during this era have been retired and replaced with newer models that have more modern conveniences. Although becoming harder to track down, these older models can still sometimes be found languishing in sheds or backyards where they probably dream of happy holidays past while they pray for restoration and a life back on the road.

Many people now look back with fondness on their early caravanning experiences and wish to re-live those happy times again. Added to that, we all share the desire for a less stressful life surrounded by beautiful things from the past, which has resulted in a huge surge in the popularity of vintage caravans and trailers during recent years. A vintage caravan provides the perfect place to indulge in some essential time out, be it on the open road, or tucked into a back garden overgrown with daisies.

Slowing down and taking time out to spend with family and friends, to explore and ponder, to visit new places, and to switch off technology so we can relax and talk to each other, is more important to people now than ever. No matter where you take it, or what the view is outside your window, relaxing in a beautifully decorated vintage trailer with a cup of tea and a good book will always feel like taking a precious step back in time to those wonderful golden years of caravanning.

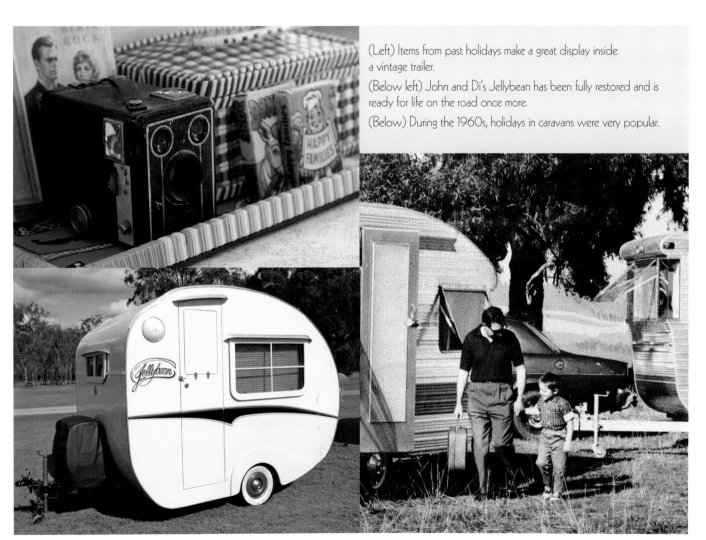

(Left) Items from past holidays make a great display inside a vintage trailer.
(Below left) John and Di's Jellybean has been fully restored and is ready for life on the road once more.
(Below) During the 1960s, holidays in caravans were very popular.

This fully restored 1960s Roadhaven was given a new lease of life and then offered as a prize at New Zealand's Beach Hop Rock 'n' Roll Festival.

We love vintage!

The interest in vintage trailers has increased dramatically over the past few years along with the renewed interest for all things 'vintage'. Be it for clothes, furniture, architecture or cars, all around the world there is a growing interest in the craftsmanship and aesthetically pleasing styles of bygone times and a shared longing for the way things used to be.

Nowadays we all live in a fast-paced world where we have become used to consuming low-quality, cheap, mass-produced goods with limited lifespans. If we can instead choose to re-use items from a time when patience and pride went into their creation, then most of us would prefer to do so; the fact that vintage products also look so much better is a bonus! The good thing about treasured old things is that if you lovingly care for them, they will continue to last for many more years to come, outliving most of their modern-day counterparts.

As we become older and even more of us find ourselves reminiscing about the old ways and the old days, mementos of these times become more and more desirable. Vintage, retro and handmade items crafted using time-honoured techniques are now more treasured than ever before. This means that in a world that continues to celebrate all things vintage and retro, a vintage caravan is right at home.

(Above left) It is hard to resist the allure of a collection of vintage wares, especially when they are housed inside a vintage trailer.

(Left) Old ice boxes, signs and thermos flasks complete this vintage trailer display.

A treasured vintage caravan will continue to provide many more years of pleasure if it is well looked after.

Taking time out

Old caravans that have been converted make the ideal place for thinking. A caravan is also just the right size to play the part of a spare room or retreat for visitors in need of some country respite, and many have been converted into dreamy backyard studios, guest rooms and retreats for teenagers, complete with cottage gardens, gnomes, plastic flamingoes and white picket fences. A vintage trailer is a wonderful place in which to escape from the world to just read and relax, indulging in glorious napping sessions that leave you feeling fully refreshed. Many people I have spoken to say that they tend to sleep even better inside a caravan than they ever do in a house.

Indeed, there is something quite special about that wonderful sense of ease and restfulness that being inside a vintage trailer creates. Whenever I take our restored vintage caravans to car shows or rallies, I always allow people right inside the van so they can experience that feeling for themselves. I love watching the smiles light up their faces, and hearing the delighted 'ooh's and 'aah's; I also love watching the surprised expression on their faces when they see how roomy and cozy these small spaces can be.

No matter what they are used for or where they go, vintage caravans seem to evoke feelings of fond nostalgia. They are great conversation starters and you will hear many comments from curious strangers such as: 'My grandparents had one of these', or 'This reminds me of that caravan we stayed in as kids way back when'.

Vintage caravans remind us all of happier, simpler times, when televisions and computers did not come on holidays, and when we shared small spaces with our family and friends – and were all OK with that. They remind us of times when we actually talked about things, introduced ourselves to our neighbours, and played board games for fun. If anyone dared utter the words 'I'm bored' then a job would soon be found to fill their idle moment, such as collecting wood for that night's fire, or peeling the potatoes.

We remember with fondness those occasions when we had time to sit, time to reflect, time to write in journals, and time to dream about who we were, what we wanted to be and where we wanted to go. Dreaming time is good for the soul, so having a specially designated dreaming space makes good sense. Now make those dreams a reality: find yourself a vintage caravan, trailer or any other small space and start creating your own dreaming space today.

(Left) Vintage caravans evoke feelings of nostalgia wherever they go.

(All right) A vintage caravan is a wonderful place in which to escape from the world, reminding us of a time when technology did not travel with us.

Let your inspiration flow

It is important to remember that there is no right or wrong when it comes to styling your space if it is expressly for your enjoyment. The photos and ideas you will find in the pages of this book are designed to inspire your inner creative spirit, which will help you to create a space that truly reflects who you are, but there are no hard and fast rules by any means. It is often said that the journey is more important than the destination, and so it goes with creating your own small space on wheels. The main thing is to enjoy the process as much as you do the end result.

After you've seen what can be done inside, and even outside, a caravan, you will hopefully be inspired to get one of your own and then decorate it. In this book you will find plenty of tips and advice so you can get started, but always seek the advice of a trained professional in trailer maintenance and repairs to look over any vintage purchase that you intend to take back out on the road, especially if it has been sitting in the middle of a field or barn for some years.

The creative aspects of restoring and decorating a vintage trailer will begin as soon as you bring it home and sit inside your newly acquired van for the first time. Allow your inspiration to flow as you imagine the colours, textures, light fittings, fixtures, curtains, cushions and flooring you will choose to fill it. That pre-decoration thinking time is a vital part of the whole process; you will spend a lot of time in this space once the work is completed, so what better place to start the process than right there inside that space?

If you are looking to develop a creative space of your own to either travel with or to stay put, a vintage caravan offers a

Mix and match textures and patterns for a lively look.

relatively affordable and easily accessible option, and their portability is an added plus! Even if you have no land to keep one on, there are plenty of storage companies in most locations that offer trailer storage options, so don't let a lack of parking space deter you from pursuing your dreams. The sense of freedom you will gain by being able to travel wherever you want, whenever you want to, will be well worth the minimal cost of storage.

The same principles and ideas that can be utilized in adding the vital finishing touches to your newly restored trailer space can be applied to the decoration of any small room or space. So if you do not own a caravan yourself and really have no plans to own one in the future, I would encourage you to find ways to incorporate these cheerful techniques into your daily living spaces, so that every day will feel like a holiday at home.

(Above left and right) Pale and pretty, or strong and vibrant — different shades reflect your personal preferences.

(All) Small details inside and out will make your space special.

A NOTE ON TERMINOLOGY

A 'caravan', as it is known in the UK, Australia and New Zealand is also known as a 'travel trailer', 'camper trailer' or just 'trailer' in the USA. As I am half Australian and half American, I tend to use these terms interchangeably depending on where I am at the time or with whom I am speaking. Some people prefer one term and many people have strong aversions to the other, so it can be difficult with a global readership to please everyone. However I have chosen to use both 'caravan' and 'trailer' interchangeably throughout this book.

Whatever you choose to call them, there is no denying that the appeal of these cozy little spaces is something that is shared by many people around the world. In my travels, I have found that there is a great sense of camaraderie amongst those who share a passion for small homes on wheels, with a very wide acceptance of differences in restorations, themes and styling. This is one interest that allows for a much greater scope of expression of uniqueness and quirkiness than many others, and is one aspect of the vintage van movement that I hope will never change. Whether owners choose to call them 'trailers' or 'caravans', they are all amazing tributes to their owner's individuality, so I think this gives owners the freedom to call their home on wheels whatever they like!

(Right) Whether their owners choose to call them 'trailers' or 'caravans', they are all amazing tributes to their owner's individuality.

Hunny Bunny Trailer

CHAPTER 2
Finding your dream caravan

(Top left) A home on wheels that would make anyone as proud as a pickle.

(Top right) An all-original interior inside this disused 1950s Winnebago.

(Above) This caravan was sold at a car show from a 'For Sale' sign in its window.

(Right) Naming your vintage trailer gives it a personality of its own.

A place to dream

The most common email enquiry I receive in my role as Editor of *Vintage Caravan Magazine* is, 'How do I find my dream vintage caravan?' After hearing so many stories about the rescue and restoration of vintage caravans and travel trailers around the world, I often reply that these retro cuties tend to find their owners, rather than the other way round. It is always a matter of being in the right place at the right time, and the stories of how people come to acquire their dream caravans are often just as interesting as the stories of how they got them back on the road.

Although there are always plenty of vans on offer on online auction and sales sites, prices are rapidly rising as demand exceeds supply and a fully restored trailer can now fetch large sums. It pays to look around for a while before rushing in and buying the first van you come across. Although it is hard not to let your heart fall in love with the rustic charms and 'cute-as' shapes of these trailers, your head needs to be very much in control of this process. The 'love at first sight' feeling can quickly diminish once you discover layers of rotting timber and a rusted chassis, subsequently finding yourself knee-deep in expensive restoration costs.

The best advice I can offer to anyone hunting for their ideal retro caravan is to become super-proactive and pester everyone and anyone you know about your dream. Tell all your friends and work colleagues, your neighbours and even the checkout girl at your local grocery store about your obsession. Older caravans are likely to pop out of the woodwork in the most unlikely places!

Faith and persistence really do make dreams come true.

Barn finds

Many a dream caravan has been rescued from the middle of a farmer's field. I know of one couple who carried out an amazing restoration on a caravan they originally spotted far away in a paddock – it even had a tree growing up through the middle of it! Unfortunately, many an old trailer has found its final resting place in a location exposed to the harshness of the elements, neglected and left to slowly disintegrate away there. Just remember that the more exposed a trailer has been over the years, the more likely it is to have suffered internal, and possibly hidden, damage, so try not to become too captivated by the desire to rescue every old van you come across. This can become an obsession!

Indeed, most of us do find it hard to stop at owning just one vintage trailer. The funny thing is that although it may seem to take forever to find even one, once you have found your dream van, all of a sudden others seem to appear everywhere you go. I now have a highly tuned 'trailer radar' that can sense the presence of a vintage trailer from several miles away – and I am not alone.

One lady I spoke to had me in hysterics as she told me her tale of 'caravans in the mist'. One morning she spotted an old aluminium, bubble-shaped caravan shrouded in thick fog far away in a farmer's paddock. She couldn't stop thinking about it all day, considering what words she would use to convince the farmer to sell it to her, without giving away how much it was worth or how passionately she wanted it. That night she said she could hardly sleep and lay awake thinking about the caravan of her dreams.

She decided that she would return the next morning with a pair of binoculars, to get a better look at the caravan and to ascertain its worth before

approaching the farmer with an offer. As she pulled up by the fence, her heart once again skipped a beat as she spotted her newfound love across the field. Yet as she peered through the binoculars and focused in on the shining aluminium bubble, she suddenly realized that the object of her desire was in fact a metal cattle feed trough! She told me that she realized then that she was becoming a little bit obsessed, but she will continue to keep looking…

However if you are lucky enough to find one, some great deals can still be made with the purchase of treasured 'barn finds'. These frozen-in-time trailers, which have been safely preserved in barns and sheds, snug and safely stored away from the harsh and destructive elements of rain, sun, wind and salt air, are still your best bet when it comes to finding a well-preserved trailer over 30 years old. Areas with relatively dry weather conditions and low humidity mean less chance of wood rot, water damage and a rusted chassis, so if you are prepared to travel a bit these drier regions are ideal spots to start your search.

(Right) The sides of old houses and sheds are good places to hunt for trailer treasure.

(Top left) Des and Kel's caravan 'Vernon' was rescued from a field where he was found with a tree growing through him. An extensive restoration saw him shining and back on the road again.

(Top right) Once your trailer radar becomes tuned in, you will start spotting unloved trailers everywhere you go.

(Above) This old abandoned Airstream sits outside the Bagdad Café in the Californian desert where it has been subject to vandalism. It is now stripped bare and full of graffiti.

(Right) This long-abandoned timber trailer was sitting far away in the middle of the desert, well off a main road in New Mexico, USA. The dry desert conditions helped to keep it well preserved with no signs of rust or rot.

Bringing it home

If you are planning on buying a long-neglected caravan, make sure you arrange for it to be towed by a professional who knows what they are doing when it comes to towing older caravans, and get it brought home or to your chosen repairer or restorer on the back of a flat-bed truck or car trailer. Never tow a caravan that hasn't been moved for three years or more, even if the registration papers have been kept up to date.

This is because no matter how good the van might look from the outside, tire rubber perishes rapidly when exposed to the elements, and wheel bearings tend to seize up if not kept in constant use. Even a short journey could turn into a disaster, adding unnecessary expenses to your restoration costs if you lose a wheel or a tire on the way home.

Moreover, if windows are missing so air can flow inside the caravan, there is a high risk that the whole caravan will literally explode off its chassis base, owing to a build up of air pressure inside the van. I have spoken to truck drivers who have insisted that I stop and pull over as soon as they noticed that one of the windows on my caravan had broken, because they have been travelling behind towed caravans and seen this happen. I didn't believe it possible at first, but these drivers spend a lot of time on the highways and have seen it all, so why take the chance?

Safety comes before aesthetics and should always be your number one priority if you plan to share the road with others. Do not risk damage to your trailer, your car, or other road users by towing an un-roadworthy trailer home and make sure you have a back-up plan in place before moving a pre-restored trailer .

(Above left) Whoever takes on this abandoned trailer as a restoration project will need to have a lot of time and money to spare!

(Far left) This sad old long trailer was spotted in a backyard, filled with piles of old junk. As it has now been built around, it will probably never move again.

(Left) An Airstream Bambi in a field in Missouri.

Shane's sheer determination to obtain the van of his dreams won out in the end.

Dreams do come true

Shane had been looking for a van for a couple of months when he discovered a 1958 Castle Windcutter advertised online. He went to take a look at it, but felt that the price being asked was too high considering the amount of work the van needed, so he walked away. A couple of weeks later he returned to take another look, but again walked away. Yet another couple of weeks went by and Shane found he couldn't stop thinking about the van, so he rang the owners again, only to find that the caravan had been sold.

By now, Shane was totally convinced that this was indeed the van of his dreams, so he asked for the buyer's phone number. The seller didn't have it, but he told Shane that the guy who had bought it lived in a semi-rural area nearby. As Shane's desire for this caravan had indeed become an obsession, he decided to take a drive to the area to see if he could find it. With visions of the Castle sitting next to a shed, he decided to start hunting around the larger acreage properties in the area.

He couldn't believe his eyes when there, on the very first street he turned down, siting next to a shed, was the caravan. It was so uncanny that Shane just knew he had to have it. He went up to the house and asked if the van was for sale; he was told 'No, definitely not'. Undeterred, Shane left his phone number with the owners, asking them to contact him if they ever decided to sell. After just a few weeks the new owners called him back to say that if Shane wanted the van he could have it; he was there within the hour with the cash.

Shane's sheer determination to obtain the van of his dreams won out in the end and his is just one of thousands of happy endings I hear about every day. So dream away, because I truly believe that when it comes to vintage trailers, dreams come true every day.

(Clockwise) Vintage trailers that are no longer in use are sometimes parked outside roadside attractions, where they make an eye-catching lure for potential customers.

Stepping inside your newly restored trailer for the first time will be one of the happiest moments of your life.

Warm and inviting, a beautifully restored vintage caravan will become a real sanctuary.

Found on an online auction site needing a bit of TLC but otherwise in working order made this New Zealand cutie a good buy.

Roll up your sleeves

Once you've found the trailer of your dreams, chances are you'll still have a long road of restoration and re-decoration ahead of you before you are ready to take it back out on the road. If you are planning to tour with your trailer, towing it over long distances, you will need to complete a fair amount of preparation to ensure that it is safe and roadworthy, that it meets all the current legislation requirements with regards to allowable towing weights, that it has up-to-date electrical and gas certificates if required, and that it is registered for road use.

If you don't intend to tow your trailer anywhere and just want to use it as a backyard studio or spare room, the restoration process is a lot simpler and much the same as renovating a room in a house. Old, cracked window rubbers and hatch seals may need to be replaced to

ensure that no rain seeps in around these areas prone to leaking, but as long as the trailer is made waterproof, the rest of the work simply involves sanding, painting, wiring and decorating.

However do be aware that a bargain is not always a bargain. Although it pains me to say it, there are some caravans that, unless you are a master builder or married to one, are quite simply beyond rescuing. Once you've restored a few trailers and realized the hours and hours of intensive labour the process involves – scrubbing, sanding, painting and sewing, replacing worn-out parts and sourcing often obsolete replacement bits and pieces – you'll realize why the fully restored or brand new replica caravans fetch the kinds of prices they do. If you are not in the least bit handy when it comes to woodwork, metal work, painting, electrics, plumbing and handicrafts, or

do not have access to someone or a team of people who are, then that bargain may well turn out to cost you a lot more than you originally bargained for in professional repairs and restoration.

The process of restoring an older trailer is very much like renovating a classic car; parts can sometimes be hard to find, and everything seems to take longer than you had planned. It is hard work, you will become dirty and cranky, and by the time you're about halfway through you will probably start wishing that you'd opted for one of those fully restored ones after all.

Having said that, if you do persevere there will come a moment when you will sit back on your newly re-upholstered dinette or on a deckchair in front of your trailer and smile to yourself, remarking that it was all worth it in the end. And that wonderful feeling will never fade away! For as much pleasure as they bring those who peek inside them at open-to-the-public displays all around the world, the greatest pleasure comes from owning one of your very own. Vintage caravans make people smile everywhere they go, and that infectious happiness is what makes their appeal so very, very enduring.

The now derelict inside of the Bagdad café Airstream brings a tear to the eye.

(Right) Restoring a vintage caravan yourself makes the end result all the more rewarding.

(Below right) Another almost perfectly preserved original interior.

(Below middle) Original replacement fittings for vintage trailers can be hard to find, so if you find spare parts that fit your trailer, grab them!

(Below) The owners of this Australian 1958 Castle Windcutter kept the interior as original as possible.

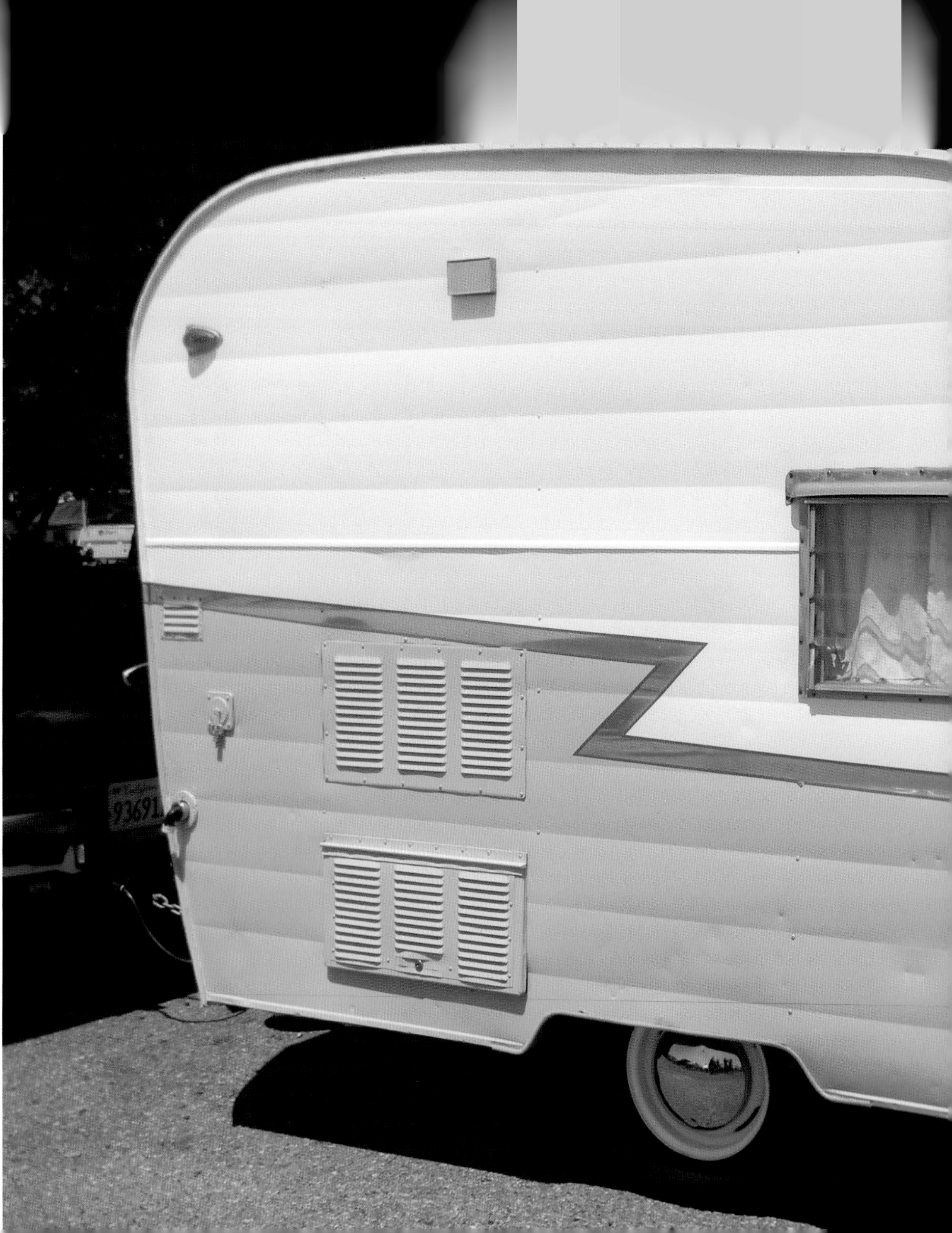

Once the hard work is all done, your restored vintage trailer will provide you with years of smiles!

Flooring

If you are lucky enough to secure a caravan with original linoleum flooring, then the best bet is to keep it intact if in good enough condition, as retro patterns and colours are highly desirable in the vintage vanning scene and are often irreplaceable. Old linoleum tiles may also contain asbestos, so if you do intend to remove them be sure not to break them as you do so.

If you do choose to replace the floor coverings in your vintage trailer, there is a great selection of new linoleum patterns, wood grain finishes, and a range of checkered flooring in a variety of colours including the ever-popular black and white checked.

Always ensure that you prepare a very clean, flat surface before you start laying tiles, as even the smallest speck of grit under your new flooring will cause a bump to appear. You can either lay your new linoleum straight over old, or create a new base using plywood. If you are laying new over the old, or onto a base from which old linoleum or tiles have been removed, make sure you sweep, sand and sugar soap the entire area to ensure the best grip.

When working out the dimensions of your floor plan, a good tip is to create a template of your floor plan by taping old pieces of newspaper together then cutting around the cupboard recesses, bed and doorway with a knife. Once you have your template, you can simply lay the joined pieces of paper over your new piece of linoleum and cut around the edges, as required.

(Left) Nothing beats the look and pattern of original retro linoleum.
(Right) Black and white checkered flooring is a popular choice in vintage caravans.

BUYER BEWARE

Five essential areas to consider when buying a vintage caravan:

RUST

A little surface rust can be easily wire-brushed and treated, but make sure that the chassis under your caravan and the drawbar that attaches it to the car are solid before you commit to buying, as replacing these essential metal parts can cost thousands.

As a desert find, this trailer would only have minimal surface rust, but you should always check for any severe rust bubbling or chipping on the underside of any trailer you consider buying.

WHEELS, TIRES AND BEARINGS

Many vintage vans have been sitting around for many years before they eventually get sold, and tire rubber deteriorates rapidly when exposed to the elements. So if there is any sign of cracking or it has been more than a few years since the van was last moved, the tires will need to be replaced and the wheel bearings may need repacking or replacing. It's always a good idea to jack the van up, remove the wheels and take them to a tire shop to get them checked before you set off anywhere.

ELECTRICS

Ask the seller if the electrics work and plug in the external power source to check the interior lights. To ensure your wiring is in line with local regulations, it is always a good idea to have it checked over by a qualified electrician. Most older caravans do not have safety switches installed and many places require you to have one in order to register your caravan or camper trailer. You will also need to check the plug that connects to your tow bar to ensure it is the same kind or if you will need an adaptor – most car parts stores stock various types of these. Some vans may have no tow bar connection at all and will therefore need to be rewired by a qualified auto electrician. As a temporary measure, a rear light bar that runs through to your tow bar can suffice, so you can safely tow the caravan to a repairer.

WATER DAMAGE

Again, a little should not put you off buying, as travelling trailers move around a lot so some form of leaking can often occur around windows or roof hatches. However just be aware that the sources of leaks can be a nightmare to find and you never know what damage water may have done to the van structurally under panels you cannot see. You may well end up rebuilding your whole caravan if the damage is extensive, so be prepared!

Plywood, Masonite or bondwood caravans and trailers can suffer wood rot within the walls if there are any signs of leaks, so fare much better if they have been stored indoors.

Aluminium caravans can also suffer water damage from perished window rubbers, rusted rivets or screws, and roof hatches that don't seal properly; signs to look for are wrinkled and raised interior ply walls and surfaces.

Laws pertaining to the use of gas inside trailers varies from place to place and can be very strict in the case of vintage appliances. A vintage trailer can be burned to the ground in less than two minutes, so always ensure your gas fittings and connections are checked by a licensed gas fitter before using them.

POTENTIALLY HAZARDOUS MATERIALS

When dealing with vehicles that were built over 30 years ago, you should be aware of the possibility that some potentially hazardous materials may have been utilized in their construction. Older paints almost always contain lead, so a mask should be worn when sanding. Older flooring tiles, stove and fridge backing boards and some interior panels can also contain asbestos, so make sure you know what you are dealing with before you start ripping into your restoration project.

CHAPTER 3
Choosing a theme

A place to express

Almost every vintage trailer owner I have ever met agrees that once you have finished any restoration or repairs required on your trailer, the fun part really begins. Up until that point ownership can just seem like a lot of hard work with little reward, and there is no doubt that restoring an older caravan or trailer can be a frustrating experience at times.

What at first may appear to be a small section of damage can often lead to a much larger repair job. Many caravans that at first seemed to need just a quick clean up can often become major restoration projects, and if you are doing most of the work yourself, it is easy to become discouraged when you look at the pile of rotted timber and removed panelling that was once your dream caravan. Indeed, when your hands are raw from sanding, your fingernails are all broken from scrubbing and your hair is full of paint, you may find yourself wondering if it is all worth it.

However once all that hard work is over, it is time to celebrate and decorate! With your blank canvas prepared, you can now express almost anything you want to, thus creating a themed space that is uniquely yours. One of the most appealing aspects of vintage trailers is their individuality. Styling and decorating these small spaces allows great scope for a variety of themes and provides an opportunity to create a space that truly reflects *your* unique tastes and style – and it is fun to do, too!

Joanne dresses to match her 1966
Kencraft's yellow theme.

(All) Add your favourite colours, fabrics
and treasures to celebrate your caravan.

It's all about you

Just remember, there is no wrong or right way to style a vintage trailer and no matter what theme you decide upon, you will find that your fellow vintage 'trailerites' are some of the most open-minded and accepting people you will ever have the pleasure of meeting. It is this acceptance of one's right to be individual that makes vintage trailer owners different from the owners of the all-white and shiny brand new models. So don't be afraid to go all out when it comes to personalizing your space.

Some people prefer to keep their trailers in exactly the same condition and colour scheme these vans had when they were first made, whereas some choose to individualize them a bit more. Either way, there will always be room enough for everyone to express themselves in whichever way they choose. Be it mild and mellow, or wild and wacky, there are as many possibilities of themes from which to choose as there are personalities in this world.

Whichever way you prefer to go really just comes down to your own personal taste. In the end, it is your caravan and you are the one that will be spending the most time in it, so follow your heart and do what *you* love. If you do choose to keep your caravan in its original style, there is still plenty of scope for individualization when it comes to decorating and accessorizing.

(Left) Don't be afraid to go all out when it comes to personalizing your own space.

(Top and bottom right) Zany or traditional— decorating a vintage trailer interior is your chance to break the rules and truly express your individuality.

Even colours that you would never normally see together can work incredibly well in a vintage van, such as the pink and red used in Kris Wade's 'Best Little Vintage Van in Vegas' in Brisbane, Australia.

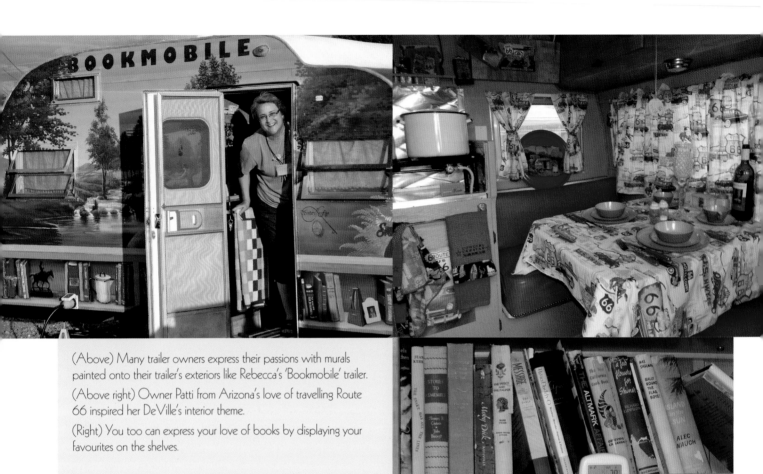

(Above) Many trailer owners express their passions with murals painted onto their trailer's exteriors like Rebecca's 'Bookmobile' trailer.

(Above right) Owner Patti from Arizona's love of travelling Route 66 inspired her DeVille's interior theme.

(Right) You too can express your love of books by displaying your favourites on the shelves.

Take your passion

The theme that you do eventually choose will form the basis of all the decisions you subsequently make with regards to styling, colour and accessories. It is therefore a good idea to spend some time thinking about this theme before you become too involved in your interior styling. From shabby chic to country and western, fishing and hunting to cowgirl style, and rock 'n' roll 1950s diner to girly floral heaven, the design possibilities for your small space are limited only by your imagination.

When looking for inspirations, think about your interests and hobbies. If you are an avid gardener with a passion for roses,

perhaps you could create a space inside your caravan that reflects these passions with a girly floral theme; at the same time, lovers of the 1950s and rock 'n' roll music may decide to use that as a basis for their theme instead. Some vintage vanners use their actual or dream location as the inspiration for their theme, and another popular inspiration is to express your vocation in your caravan.

I know of one lady librarian in the USA who decided to incorporate her love of books into her trailer theme; she had murals of books painted all over the outside of her trailer and this looked simply sensational.

AN INSPIRATION BOARD

If you are struggling to choose a theme, try creating an inspiration board to start the creative juices flowing. This is a device often used by creatives, and comprises a collection of images and materials that inspire you or make you feel good. An inspiration board will ultimately prove a great help in guiding your decisions when it comes to choosing a theme based around things that interest you; in the words of Irene Cara, 'take your passion and make it happen'.

To make an inspiration board: take a large piece of cardboard then glue to it a selection of favourite photos, pictures found in magazines and on the Internet, colour charts from hardware stores, pieces of fabric, and anything else you can find that strikes a chord with you. Once complete, position your board on a wall where you can look at it every day, and add to it whenever you see something visual that peaks your interest. With all the elements of your interests brought together on the board, before long a consistent theme will appear.

Collecting all your ideas together on a pin board or computer will help to inspire a theme.

Hollywood glamour

Stan and Debbie are huge fans of the classic 1950s Hollywood movie stars. So when they decided to call their polished aluminium trailer 'Marilyn', the theme soon fell securely into place. The entire wall behind the dinette is adorned with a collage of black and white Marilyn Monroe images, Marilyn memorabilia abounds inside the caravan, and a flag with an image of Marilyn flaps happily from the flagpole. Avid rock 'n' rollers, even Stan's classic 1960s car is painted off-white with ghost flames that complement the black and white theme they have chosen to use inside the caravan. Once you've chosen a theme, it seems to be that items that work with this will appear everywhere – and your friends will always know what to get you for gifts!

Shabby chic

When it comes to choosing a theme for the decoration of vintage caravans, it is hard to resist the allure and charm of country cottage style, which has come to be known as 'shabby chic'. This eclectic blending of florals, ginghams, polka dots and stripes in either bold primary colours or muted pastel tones works perfectly in small spaces, creating a cozy and charming yesteryear feel that is ideally suited to vintage caravans. Crochet granny blankets are the best accessories to have in a vintage trailer and the ultimate in shabby chic cool so, if you still remember how, get out those crochet needles and start making some blankets in colours that are just right for your theme.

Lucy Jayne Grout from West Sussex in the UK perfected the art of creating unique, country-styled interiors in her vintage style interiors business, which sold painted furniture along with quirky and unusual retro-styled homewares and accessories. Family holidays used to be taken in the family's VW Campervan until her husband suggested that a caravan might be a better solution to provide the family with a bit more room. 'We looked at a few newish ones, but I could not stand all the plastic and velour!' says Lucy. 'I agreed we should get a caravan, but only if I could have an old one and be surrounded by all my vintage bits and bobs.' Lucy has now turned her talents and her passion to restoring and decorating beautiful bespoke caravans for others with her business, *Lucy Jayne Caravans*.

Gypsy romance

A custom-restored vintage trailer is your mobile escape on wheels – be it on the road, or stationary. For many of us, being inside a van transports us back to a time in history when gypsies roamed the countryside in brightly coloured and elaborately decorated 'vardos' or caravans. Decorating your own trailer is a perfect opportunity to channel and celebrate your inner gypsy. Schultz and Carol are from California, and the gypsy theme works really well in their 1963 Silverstreak named 'Brigitte Vardo'.

This romantic, olden-day look can be achieved in your own vintage van with deep and luxurious reds, mixing and matching textures such as velvet, fur, lace and satin. Add crystal chandeliers and delicate fine china items to adorn the table and shelves – just make sure you have a box full of bubble wrap to pack them away when you are on the road! Think richness, grandeur, romance and adventure when choosing your colours, and accessories that evoke the mystery and intrigue of this look.

Original retro

Of course, one theme that will always make complete sense is original retro, styling your trailer's interior in keeping with the era of its build date. Should you choose to maintain the interior of your caravan as close to the original as possible, sticking to an as-it-would-have-been-back-in-the-day theme will work really well. There is still plenty of room for individualization, as the possibilities for using genuine retro kitchenalia and fittings and fixtures right down to the fabric of the curtains and pastel-based colour schemes are endless.

Even an outdoor studio, cabin, room of a house or garage can be converted to a step-back-in-time capsule using easily sourced items from an earlier era, now restored to their former glory. Antique and thrift stores, swap meets and garage sales are good places to source items that were made around the same time as your trailer, and these will often inspire you in your choice of theme. Think chenille bedspreads, Bakelite storage canisters and old board games, toys, books and trinkets to really embrace this original retro theme with success.

Rock 'n' roll diner

The bold primary colours and the black and white check-tiled flooring used in 1950s American diners work really well with the retro laminates, shiny vinyl upholstery and chrome trims often found in old trailers. Accentuate your chosen colour scheme with gingham curtains and

rock 'n' roll themed decorations, with the addition of old records on the wall and tributes to your favourite 1950s recording artists. You will find plenty of inspiration in retro shops and antique stores if you wish to recreate this fun and cheerful atmosphere inside your caravan.

For girly girls

For many women, decorating a vintage caravan is a chance to really embrace their girly side and create a truly feminine retreat. Floral themes, vases of roses and shades of pink all contribute to the ambience of rest and relaxation, and can work really well inside any small space.

Decorating a caravan or trailer allows you to create a dreamy interior that is conducive to long cups of tea, relaxing with a good book and indulging in long naps. Allow your caravan to become your own personal grown-up cubby house and fill it with as many pretty things as you can find to let the stresses of the world just melt away.

For example, Elaine from California's 1963 Shasta 'My Pink Wings' is a tribute to her survival from breast cancer and a celebration of being a woman. Her use of delicate florals and shades of pink both inside and out really expresses her youthful, cheerful and optimistic personality well.

Hot rod heaven

A lot of people who own vintage caravans also own custom cars or hot rods and choose to theme their caravans to match their cars. Hot rodding is about taking something stock standard and making it even better. In cars this may mean a bigger engine, a roof chop, pin striping or the addition of chrome trims, flame paint jobs and customized bodywork to make the vehicle truly unique. Over the years vintage trailers have become the ultimate car show accessory where they serve as accommodation for avid car show travellers, so a matching hot rod and trailer makes for a real head-turning combo as it cruises down the highway.

   To recreate this theme you will need to think about chrome accessories, lots of shiny two-pack paintwork and the addition of extra bits of 'bling', such as an added bumper from an old car or a decorative spare wheel mount. Mike from New Zealand went all out on his 1960s caravan using parts that he sourced over the years from swap meets. He even polished up an old set of drive-in movie speakers that hook onto the outside of the van and connect up to his iPod to create the ultimate party space at hot rod shows.

The great outdoors

Many people still use their trailers to take on outdoor pursuits such as hunting, horse riding and fishing trips, so they choose a theme that celebrates their passion for the great outdoors. Avid fisherwoman Debbie's 1949 home-built trailer is named 'Tackle Box' and contains plenty of fishing-inspired decorations inside. The good thing about using your passion as the basis for your style theme is that you will probably already have plenty of items relating to that interest collected over the years, which will help transform your trailer into a travelling museum of the things you love.

Wild, Wild West

Some people choose to date the interior styling of their trailers to before these vehicles were made, to create a rustic Western theme that evokes scenes of cowboys and Indians on the Wild West frontiers. Deborah named her 1966 Aloha 'Annie Oakley 'n' Me' and has used plenty of timber finishes on the cupboard doors and floor to evoke that Wild West theme. Cowhide trims and leather have been used in the upholstery and the curtains are made from hessian sackcloth and old lace. Outside, the oilskin canvas awning is held up with old tree branches and an old copper bath adds to the rustic yesteryear charm.

Rockabilly kitsch

If you love all things retro, owning a vintage trailer allows you to embrace your inner 'trailer trash' and recreate the tackiest aspects of 1950s and 1960s styling. I love pink flamingos, kitsch ceramic ornaments, hula girls and pinup art, Rockabilly music and dancing – in fact, all things Rockabilly from the 1950s and early 60s. Thus the pink trimmed cabinets and black and white flooring of my 1964 Australian Sunliner were the basis for my style focus, to which I added red and white polka-dot curtains, plastic hibiscus leis and plenty of brightly coloured anodized canisters, along with my travel postcards on the walls. What I have ended up with is a theme I now call 'Gidget's Hawaiian holiday meets Barbie's pink campervan'; she certainly makes people smile whenever she is on display at shows! Inside Betty Page-Turner's soft pink, fibreglass exterior is a busy, brightly coloured and a little bit crazy interior; although it might not be to everyone's taste, it is totally 'me'.

It's all about the style

Picking a theme based on your unique personality and interests makes the whole styling process flow much more easily and provides you with a space in which you will always feel right at home.

Thus all of these retro themes can be just as easily applied to styling and decorating any small space that you are lucky enough to have to set aside as a designated retreat, such as cabins, garages, attics and holiday houses, as well as caravans and camper trailers.

And don't forget the outside! Having a theme that spills out of the door, under the awning and into the space around the trailer makes for stunning open-to-public displays at classic car shows and vintage trailer rallies.

(Above far left) Creating a cozy space does not have to be limited to trailers.

(Above left) Caravans create that holiday feeling wherever they are situated.

(Bottom far left) This quirky collection of kitsch items looks great displayed around the caravan's doorway.

(Left) Vintage caravans make great holiday homes.

(Above) Make visitors to your trailer feel welcome by creating an inviting entranceway.

(Left) Using ideas and colours from retro hostelries such as the Blue Swallow Motel on Route 66 will help inspire the decoration in your holiday home.

CHAPTER 4

Choosing a colour scheme

A place to colour

When it comes to choosing a colour scheme for your vintage trailer, the vast spectrum of possibilities is as wide as the rainbow's end is impossible to find. Some people prefer to use the trailer's original colours as the basis for their palette, while many others sand everything back to the base surface and start all over again with their own scheme. Choosing a colour scheme based on the predominant original colours of your trailer or your favourite colours is always the best place to start, and you will find that accessorizing becomes easy once you have chosen a base palette to work with.

Nobody will know better what colours you will feel most comfortable spending time with than you, so feel free to go all out with your choice of colours, both inside and outside your vintage trailer. I have seen caravans decorated in every scheme, from muted heritage colours of cream, russet red and forest green, to bright and bold red, black and white like an American diner, to absolutely adorable pink palaces with mint green accents – they all look absolutely fabulous. As long as *you* love the colour scheme you choose, it will always work well. In fact, I've yet to see a colour scheme in a caravan that I didn't like.

(All) Bright, bold colours and patterns or soft pastels create an individual holiday vibe inside a vintage caravan.

Lighter colours such as white create the illusion of more space and can be accented with whatever colour makes you feel good.

Colour therapy

There is plenty of information out there about the psychology of colour and how different colours can affect mood, health and even relationships. If you are having trouble deciding between different colour schemes then why not carry out a bit of research into the effect of colours to see if that helps you make your decision?

Darker, warmer colours such as reds and maroons are said to get the blood pumping and can create a luxurious, intimate aura in a small space. By contrast, shades of light blue have been found to be more calming and relaxing, and some studies show that light blue walls can actually reduce blood pressure.

Yellow is often perceived as a happy, cheery colour that we relate to sunny summer holidays, so this can be a popular choice in the colour schemes of older vans and trailers. Meanwhile orange and citrus shades are bold and bright, and are said to induce feelings of energy and excitement.

Of course, these examples are not true for all people and nobody really understands the reason why some colours please our eyes more than others. The important thing to remember is that whichever colours you choose, they should be the ones that you find easy to live with and that make you feel most at ease.

(Above left) Colour coordinating with yellow accessories brings the whole theme together in Joanne's 1966 Kencraft.

(Left) Colour schemes can revolve around the entire spectrum of shades.

(Left) Black, white and red are so very rock 'n' roll.

(Below) Nicole's 1948 Bondwood named 'Ruby' is finished in the traditional colours of red and cream.

(Bottom right) Orange interiors create a cheerful vibe.

(Bottom left) The striking red and white colour scheme of Alan and Jaysa's 1966 Aladdin has seen it win many awards at trailer rallies.

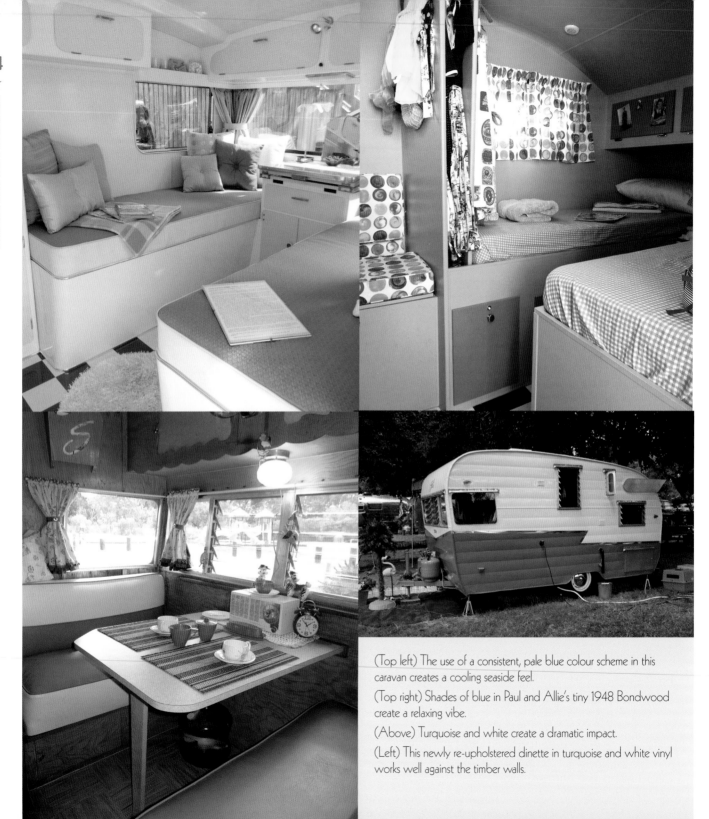

(Top left) The use of a consistent, pale blue colour scheme in this caravan creates a cooling seaside feel.

(Top right) Shades of blue in Paul and Allie's tiny 1948 Bondwood create a relaxing vibe.

(Above) Turquoise and white create a dramatic impact.

(Left) This newly re-upholstered dinette in turquoise and white vinyl works well against the timber walls.

Some people prefer a monochrome colour scheme which creates a less cluttered and cleaner look inside their small spaces.

John and Glenda Chapman's
1938 Chev pickup and 1950s
homemade caravan.

A very cool combo

Many people choose to tow their retro caravans behind newer, more reliable vehicles; if you prefer to do this it's totally fine and nobody will think less of you – lots of vintage vanners do this. However nothing looks cooler than a matching retro trailer and classic car combination cruising down the road. Should you be lucky enough to own a 'matching set', you'll know that these era-matched pairs make an impact wherever they travel and are guaranteed to start cameras snapping!

Retro trailers and caravans are often painted to match their classic tow cars, especially for weekend-long hot rod runs and car shows.

(Above) Brad and Lisa chose a green colour scheme for their 1961 Charlwyn to match their green 1958 Plymouth Belvedere.

(Above right) Bob and Maria's Model A hot rod and colour matched caravan have travelled extensively all around Australia.

(Right) Chris Schultz made this replica retro caravan to match his classic wagon.

Re-painting a trailer in shiny two-pack paint will still cost a lot less than re-spraying a whole car, so often the trailer receives the re-paint to match the car, rather than the other way around. Chrome trims to match the car can also be added to the trailer to achieve a really coordinated and truly vintage look.

Brad and Lisa chose their 1961 Charlwyn caravan because they were looking for the ultimate accessory for their two-toned green 1958 Plymouth Belvedere car to take to car shows and events. They found the caravan for sale online, and when they went to see it they knew straight away that it was the one – they drove it home the same day. As Brad explained, 'The main reason we bought it was because of its green interior. The outside didn't matter so much because I knew I could paint that, but the inside was already green and so it was perfect just as it was.' Apart from a small repair required in the back corner, the marine-ply-over-timber-frame caravan was in near perfect condition when they bought it. Once the repair was done, all that was required was to paint the exterior of the caravan in contrasting moss and emerald greens and fill it with retro accessories.

TIPS FOR PAINTING YOUR VAN

Some essential tips for re-decorating your caravan:

WATER DAMAGE

Water damage will soon undo all your hard work unless it is repaired before you start to paint. The culprits that can cause internal moisture to build up between the exterior cladding and the internal walls include perished and cracked window rubbers, rusted nails in the exterior cladding and worn out rivets. Carefully check for all these, and repair or replace them wherever you can; also repair and waterproof any holes or cracks you find.

PREPARATION

As with any painting job, preparation is key, so be prepared to spend plenty of time cleaning, sanding and puttying old holes long before the first coat of paint goes on. Thoroughly scrub clean any surfaces prior to sanding and painting with sugar soap to remove grease, smoke or road grime. Many pre-1980 caravans may have also been previously painted with lead-based paints, so be sure to wear a mask when sanding old paintwork.

PRIMING

The walls of many caravans, especially those built in the 1960s and 1970s, are clad in a high-gloss laminex sheeting and paint does not adhere well to this. If painting over laminated cupboards or walls, make sure you sand the surface until it is rough then use a special bonding preparation coat to prime the surface so your paintwork doesn't scratch right off.

PAINTING

Any auto paint shop should be able to re-spray a trailer in any colour you choose, and if you want a professional looking finish then it does pay to employ professionals to carry out this work for you. For those whose budgets don't extend to a professional two-pack paint job, heavy duty gloss acrylic house paint can be watered down and sprayed with a compressor, or applied with a roller, onto the caravan; although the paint finish will not last as long, look as good, or ever be as shiny as a professional job.

POLISHING

If your trailer is made of unpainted aluminium cladding, a good polishing with plenty of elbow grease and a substance such as Purple Polish will return it to a gleaming silver shine.

Some people prefer to retain the faded original paintwork on their trailer for that genuine vintage patina look.

Paul and Allie's blue 1948 Bondwood caravan is towed by their matching blue 1965 Holden Special.

CHAPTER 5
Decorating your caravan

A place to style

Once your theme and colour scheme have been chosen, you can start thinking about the soft furnishings you'd like to have inside your fresh new space. This is when your theme will really start to become apparent, as the 'skin' is laid over the (hopefully by then) well restored 'bones' of the 'being' that your trailer will by now have become.

Most owners have named their acquisition by the time they bring it home, but if you haven't done so by now, this is a good time to choose a name and start creating the basis of what will become your van's personality. It always pays to have a nicely cleansed and newly restored shell to work with when styling, so thoroughly scrub clean any original surfaces that are left so the van truly feels yours.

(All) Once you've scrubbed and decorated the main parts of your space, have fun hanging or grouping together items to achieve a greater impact.

(Left) Brad and Lisa's love of Rockabilly and the colour green inspired their choice of interior.

(Right) Wrought iron outdoor settings are right at home outside a pretty vintage caravan.

Take
a seat

By the time you come across your old trailer, the padding materials inside its upholstered seats and mattresses will have spent a long time collecting dust mites and other unsavoury particles; in addition, some of the older upholstery would have been made with coconut fibres or even horsehair inserts. This means that, as much as I love the original aspects of vintage trailers, these are the sort of things that could use an update to their more comfortable and hygenic modern versions.

The original upholstery used in dinette seats is often worn, faded or ripped and does tend to harbour nasty musty smells, so I recommend having new foam rubber cut to size and replacing it from scratch. There is a huge variety of long-wearing vinyl finishes that are ideal for caravan upholstery and any car upholsterer should be able to make these up for you, with a nicely contrasting piping or button finish.

Alternatively, you may prefer to use a more traditional upholstery fabric and make use of the vast array of patterns and colours available in these fabrics. If you are handy with a sewing machine, you can cover your seats yourself in any fabric you choose. If your budget doesn't extend to new upholstery, a homemade granny blanket draped across the seats along with piles of coordinating cushions works well, too.

(All) Replacing worn and musty old upholstery is always a good idea.

Framing the view

When decorating small spaces such as caravans, cubby houses or studios, curtains play a vital role, providing frames to those beautiful views that you will most likely be looking out across if you choose to take your retro rolling home out to explore the big, wide world. When inside your caravan, your eye will be drawn to the view outside your window and the light flowing into your surprisingly bright and sunny space. In confined spaces the curtains will be the most obvious element of your whole interior style, so they have to be right.

As much as I love the 'busyness' of my caravan's interior, some very small spaces can appear too busy and cluttered by hanging curtains that have too many colours or patterns. Gingham checks, polka dots and simple florals work really well, and some people even prefer the simplicity of venetian blinds. However when it comes to recreating a genuine retro style, nothing beats the look of genuine bark cloth fabric for vintage trailer curtains.

Luckily curtains for a trailer are really easy to sew up yourself, being essentially rectangles of fabric with seams at the sides and hems at the top and the bottom, the top hem being the one through which the curtain elastic or doweling passes. Once you have made one curtain to measure, the rest can be patterned from the one that has been completed so all the curtains are equal in size.

At night, when the interior lights are on, it is nice to have curtains that will allow a pleasant light to pass through them, and I love the pink glow that the light shining through my red and white polka-dot curtains creates. As pleasant as light coloured and white or lace curtains may be, make sure they are thick enough to not be transparent in the dark caravan park at night when you are getting undressed. Alternatively hang two layers of curtains: one sheer or lacy fabric that lets the light in but provides some privacy during the day and another row of thicker curtains over the top that can be drawn closed at night. Block-out backing fabric, roller blinds or double-sided curtains provide complete privacy at night and are ideal if you want complete darkness at any time.

(All) Choose your curtains and hang them with pride! Pink pinup style cowgirl curtains (below left) were just right in this western themed trailer; meanwhile polka dots (right) create a cheerful atmosphere inside Lucy Jayne's vintage caravan.

A cushy ride

I am a big fan of cushions, as they are the ultimate cozy space accessory. I have mountains of them all over my bed and across the back of my dinette seats. Indeed, when I go to bed it can take a while to remove the piles of cushions from the bed so there is room for me to sleep! In my travels I have seen a wonderful array of methods to personalize and use cushions in vintage trailers and caravans. Not only do they make your lounging experience so much more comfortable, they also add a dash of colour and texture to your décor, which can be altered at a moment's notice as your tastes change without the need to renovate.

Like curtains, cushions are relatively easy to make and there are some great retro styles and fabrics to be found. Update recycled materials, or source retro patterns and colours from the larger fabric and haberdashery stores, which also usually stock pre-fabricated cushion inserts in set sizes. Then appliqué cut-out shapes in other fabrics onto your homemade cushions to create a one-of-a-kind focal feature that fits your theme just perfectly. New Zealander Beth used appliqué over old woollen checked blankets to create cozy cushions for the gelato coloured interior of her 1966 Silverstream.

(All) Cushions add a dash of colour and help create a warm and cozy space inside a vintage van.

Accessorize it!

Just about everyone I have spoken to about their trailers agrees that accessorizing your space is the best part of the whole restoration process. Once the hard work of sanding, painting, sewing curtains and laying of flooring has been done, the placement of ornaments, retro memorabilia, pictures, signs, bunting and other bits and pieces is what will make your home away from home really stand out from the crowd.

Most of us started collecting little knick-knacks and retro objects for years before these made their way into our caravans. Chances are you already have objects around your home that could be incorporated into your small space interior but if not, searching for vintage and retro items online or in antique stores and garage sales is a great way to start your collection.

Keep an eye out for anodized and Bakelite canisters, ceramic ornaments and vases, other kitchen items and even old books, magazines and games that will create a feeling of old world nostalgia inside your caravan. Even the addition of a freshly picked bunch of garden flowers displayed in a retro vase will add a touch of yesteryear charm to your caravan's interior; fake flowers work well, too!

Whether you use it for holidaying, as a backyard studio, or open your doors to others at car shows and rallies, a selection of quirky retro items in your chosen colour scheme can be displayed both inside and outside your trailer to great effect. Vintage trailers provide the ideal portable museum for you to display all of your salvaged 'trailer treasures'.

(All) A vintage caravan is a great place to display your collection of retro wares.

Keeping it shady

If you are very lucky, you may discover the original annexes, poles, ropes and pegs in a drawer inside your old van. If not, there are quite a few options when it comes to creating a unique awning, if you have access to an industrial sewing machine and some good weather-resistant fabric.

If you do not have access to an industrial sewing machine or know someone who does, you can still get a custom-made awning at many heavy-duty upholsterers or caravan awning makers. Some weatherproof awning canvases can be sourced from online suppliers, and your local upholsterer may well even sew it up to your measurements if you ask nicely. If they won't create the fancy scalloped edges and fringed tassles, don't despair, you can still create a very pretty effect by stringing bunting and fairy lights along the edges of your awning instead.

In addition, there are companies popping up now around the world who are beginning to realize the demand for retro-styled awnings and annexes for restored retro trailers. Some post their made-to-order awnings made from candy striped canvas all around the world at fairly reasonable prices, which do often come complete with tassled fringing and scalloped edges. These awnings look great supported by traditional wooden tent poles and rope if you can find them, although I actually find that telescopic aluminium poles travel much more easily.

(Below) This awning was cleverly made by sewing the pockets of old denim jeans together.

(Above left) Mandy had her set of red striped awnings custom made to fit her 1963 Capricorn caravan.

(Above right) Striped awnings and scalloped edges will complete the retro look of your vintage trailer.

(Above) Tassle fringes and scalloped edges give your awning a very retro look.

(Left) Chris and Julie were lucky enough to get their Viscount's original 1960s awning when they bought the caravan.

We love bunting!

For the final finishing touches, you can't do better than the delightful and cheery atmosphere that strings of well-placed bunting can provide. I just love bunting: I have it inside my caravans, I hang it on the outside of my caravan and string it along the outside of my awnings; I even have it hanging around in my home. Bunting or party flags make every day seem like a celebration, and the variety of fabrics and materials used to create this joyful decoration is endless.

Make bunting from the same fabrics and colour schemes used in other aspects of your interior, such as cushions or upholstery, then hang this around the caravan exterior –

this is a great way to extend your chosen theme from the inside out. Or string together a collection of the old souvenir pennant flags that you used to be able buy in every town you visited to make a fascinating travel themed bunting.

Bunting flags can be easily made using a length of bias binding from a haberdashery store with small triangles of fabric sewn inside the binding. I have seen old lace doilies cut in half to create a string of delicate bunting in a mostly white interior, and it looked absolutely amazing. You can also use old handkerchiefs, fabric off-cuts from your craft projects, and even paper and string bunting works really effectively, too.

TRAILER OF LOVE

Mike and Jeanette's 3-metre (10-foot) 1966 Shasta Compact was a wedding gift from their friends who all contributed money to buy and restore it for them. When I met the couple, they had slept in it for the very first time the previous night. The exterior of the cute little lemon yellow and white trailer is draped in the crafty bunting their friends also made to decorate the trailer when they gave it to the newlyweds as a gift. Simply made from paper and string, each flag is inscribed with words of love and encouragement to the happy couple, written by their friends in their own handwriting.

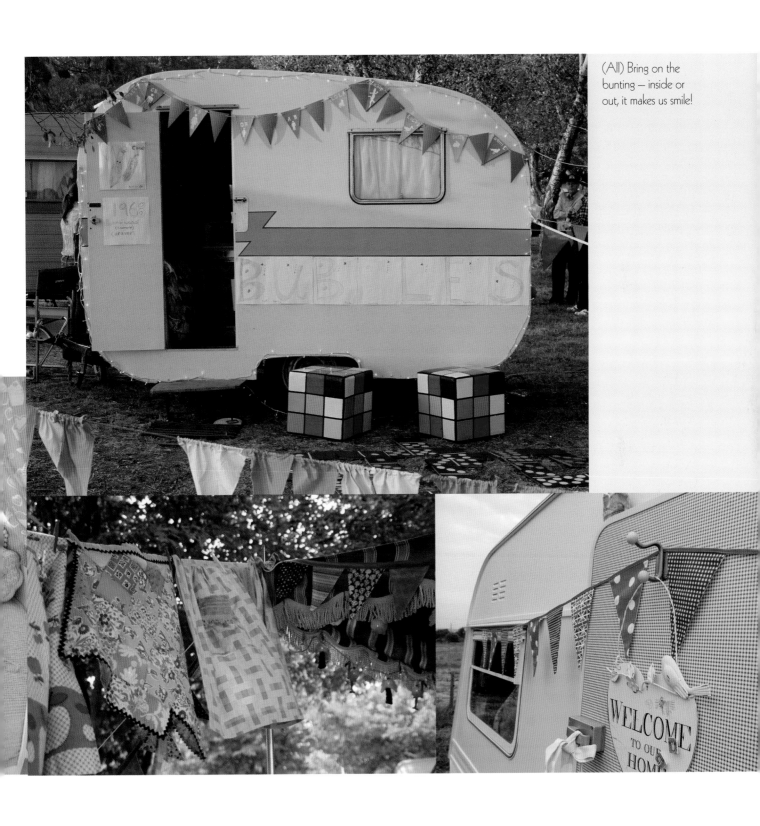

(All) Bring on the bunting — inside or out, it makes us smile!

(All) Bright and cheerful bunting flags can be made from any fabric leftovers you may have from making curtains and cushions, or even from recycled old handkerchiefs or doilies.

(This page) Flamboyant flamingoes, trailer wind chimes, matching bikes and blinged-up number plates add panache to the outside area of your trailer.

Take it outside

Speaking of indoors and outdoors, you will need to start thinking about gathering a collection of theme-appropriate outdoor accessories to provide your campsite with a real the-way-we-were look. Suitable items can still be sourced second-hand from plenty of thrift or antique stores, and these look great propped up against the outside of either an on-site caravan or at an open-to-the-public display at a car show or trailer rally.

Think about what kinds of items may have been seen at a campsite back in your trailer's hey-day: retro bicycles and outdoor furniture, old ice boxes, iconic plastic pink flamingos, garden gnomes, flower boxes and old wireless radios are all good choices when it comes to selecting appropriate props for your retro display.

(Above) Window boxes create that extra detail that says 'home'.
(Right) Garden gnomes make excellent flamingo bodyguards.

CHAPTER 6

Taking a road trip

A place to explore

If your ambition has been to use your newly restored, decorated and accessorized trailer for what it was designed to do – to take you on adventurous road trips to beautiful locations – then you'll no doubt be itching to get on the road with your rig. By now your trailer will have taken on so much of its own personality that you will swear it gives you the same kind of look that a dog does when it wants a walk – it will love the fun of a road trip just as much as you do. Obviously there are a few tips to bear in mind before setting out on any road trip, especially for first timers:

- It is always a good idea to arrange for your tow car to be serviced before departure, and let the mechanics know that you intend to use it for towing.
- Before any long trip check your wheel bearings and tires, especially if it has been a while since the van was used to go anywhere. If you've recently fitted new wheels, double check that all the wheel nuts are tight.

- Before you travel too far down the road, check the pressure in all the tires of your car and caravan, including the spares. Always carry a spare wheel for both your trailer and car, and learn how to change a flat; if you don't know how to do this then ask someone to show you.
- Sway bars, weight distribution bars or load levellers to ensure the weight

from the drawbar to the tow ball is evenly distributed across the car make handling and braking more reliable, and also diminish the swaying that can occur whilst being overtaken by a large truck. Although not legally required, these are a good investment for a smoother ride.
- Batten down the hatches! Before you set off, make sure all the windows and

(All) Size does matter – make sure you check the legal towing capacity of your tow car and know what size of caravan you can comfortably tow whatever highway you plan to travel.

the ceiling hatch are closed and firmly secured in their latches, and that your extra door latch is in place. In addition, always make sure all your retro knick-knacks are safely bubble wrapped and stored away in boxes before you set off, as the trailer will bump around and things will move inside.

- Cut a spare key for the caravan and keep it on a lanyard around your neck at all times during your travels. You'll understand why this is important the first time you get locked out of your van during one of those midnight trips to the amenities block.
- Be brave! Although there is safety in numbers when travelling in convoy with other

vintage caravanners, don't allow being a solo traveller stop you from getting out there and exploring. I quite often venture out on caravan trips on my own and have found other travellers more than welcoming and friendly out there on the road.

- A two-way radio, a good mobile phone, membership to a nationwide automobile club that offers roadside assistance including towing for both car and caravan, and a decent GPS will get you through most of the precarious scenarios that occur on the road.

Enjoy the wide open spaces of the road with your vintage trailer in tow.

Packing essentials

Once you've taken a few major road trips, you'll soon realize that the odd mishap will happen along the way – but it need not ruin your fun. As long as you are well prepared for all contingencies, you will find that dealing with minor hiccups is all part of it.

About a week before you set off on an extended road trip, start a list of things you need to remember to pack and keep adding items as you remember them. Keep this list by your bed so you can jot down those important things you only seem to remember as you drift off to sleep. When you pack your van, tick items off as you go.

Also, set aside one cupboard or drawer in your van for a tool kit and always have a set of the following items on hand inside: a hammer; a cordless drill and battery charger with drill bits and drivers; a rivet gun and rivets, if you have an aluminium van; silicone and a caulking gun for sealing any possible leaks; a selection of screws, nuts and bolts, and slip pins in various sizes; a large roll of duct tape, which is fantastic for emergency window repairs; and a roll of wire and set of pliers, excellent for temporary fixes on broken brake cable.

Other things to pack include:

- Awning, ropes and tent pegs as well as a rubber hammer.
- An emergency tarpaulin.
- Plenty of water for both you and the car.
- Long life milk if you are restricted for space in the fridge or ice box.
- At least three towels for each person – one for the shower, one for the beach and one old one for the floor to stop muddy footprints inside the van.
- A storage box with plenty of bubble wrap for all your retro breakables during transit.
- A caravan electrical cord, waste and fresh water hoses and connectors.

The rest is up to you and depends largely on where you are going and what you intend to do, but pack for a normal camping trip.

WHAT NOT TO PACK

I'm as guilty as the next person of this and have only recently mended my ways and cleared out my caravan cupboards of several tins of food that were probably way past their use-by dates. Unless you really, really like canned baked beans or spaghetti, don't pack them; the chances are they will just end up sitting in the cupboard of your trailer adding unnecessary weight. Speaking of which, any heavy items such as outdoor furniture, awnings and such are best packed in the car rather than in the trailer, as it is safer for a heavier car to tow a lighter trailer rather than the other way around.

(Far left) Retro picnic sets and iceboxes remind us of holidays from the past.

(Right) Be conscious of carrying excess weight in your caravan and limit pantry items to those you know you will actually use.

Hitching up

If you've had plenty of experience in driving and parking trailers, boats or horse floats, then this will all seem a bit basic. However it is worth having some kind of system in place to ensure that you complete all the necessary steps when it comes to the important task of connecting or disconnecting your caravan to your car, as the consequences of missing one vital step in the process could be potentially catastrophic and cause extensive damage to your trailer or another driver. Similar to rock climbing, you need to check to make sure that all of the back up systems are in place and engaged. Hooking up your trailer to the car, reverse parking it into a campsite space and unhitching are some of the things that can seem a bit daunting at first to people who have had little or no experience. But with a few smart tips, a bit more awareness and plenty of practice you will master these things in no time. If not, there will always be some nearby camper to lend a hand if need be.

When backing up to the drawbar to hitch the van up by myself, I will often put the car in park, leave the engine running then jump out to see how far left, right and back I need to go. It's perfectly fine to get out to check and correct this as many times as you need to, and it becomes easier the more you do it. Backing up a trailer is easier with a newer car that has power steering; it can be a bit more challenging with older cars, but if you just remember to repeat the word 'opposite' to yourself, you'll find the process so much more logical! In other words, if you want the rear end of your caravan behind you to veer to the right, you steer as if you wanted to turn left, and vice versa; the more left you steer, the more right swing the van will take. Several corrected manoeuvres are better than any hard left or right steers, if you want to avoid jackknifing the whole set up, possibly causing damage to the car or trailer. When it comes to hitching and unhitching, safety should be your priority.

I have a system I call JCHE – not a particularly good acronym or anything, but I repeat this sequence of letters whenever I hitch or unhitch my caravan to the car, to remind me to check all the hitching mechanisms are secure:

- J = Jockey Wheel. First make sure the jockey wheel has been locked back up and out of the way.
- C = Chain. The next step is to make sure the safety chain on the drawbar and D-shackle are correctly connected to the tow bar on the car.
- H = Handbrake. Once you are satisfied that the tow ball and coupling are securely locked in and the chain is fastened, release the handbrake.
- E = Electrics. Plug the electrical cord into the car's socket and run a check on the trailer brake and indicator lights to make sure they are all working properly.

Whenever you back the car up to the van and hook it all up it pays to make yet another check over the JCHE system before driving away. When unhitching, work through the same sequence but this time putting the jockey wheel down, releasing the chain, engaging the handbrake and undoing the plug from the socket on the car before winding the jockey wheel up until the tow coupling on the trailer releases the tow ball so you can move the car away.

(All) Taking the time to hitch up correctly will keep you and your precious trailer safe.

It's a wild world

Travelling across the countryside in a vintage trailer will have you slowing down and appreciating the scenery in a way you will have never experienced before, especially if you are towing with an older car. Luckily I have noticed that other road users seem more than understanding of your need to comfortably cruise at 80kph (50mph) should they see that your old caravan is being towed by an old car. Alas, the same cannot be said for drivers who see that you have a new car towing your old van.

Be very aware on the roads, as some drivers can be quite aggressive about caravans slowing things down and may cut you off, or dangerously overtake if you choose to meander along. The main thing is to drive calmly and graciously in what would be described as a defensive manner. Understand that having a large, solid item behind your car creates a potential hazard on the road and drive cautiously, with an even greater sense of awareness of your wider, longer load and where other road users are around you at all times. If you can't see beyond your trailer, then you may want to think about installing towing mirrors on your car to provide a wider view.

THE CODE

It should go without saying – but I will say it anyway. If you are out there travelling this big wide world of ours, enjoying the freedom of the open road and the beauty of our natural environment, then please respect it. Take only photographs and leave only footprints.

Don't leave any of your rubbish behind anywhere you stop, and carry a bag with you in the car in which to toss any garbage so you can take it with you to dispose of properly. There are plenty of rest areas with amenities out on the road, so please try not to make a mess anywhere else!

Be nice to other travellers. It doesn't matter if they have a brand new shiny giant trailer or a homemade wooden teardrop, if they are out there sharing the road with you then give them a wave. If you were in trouble they'd stop and help you; you should try to do the same, as long as you feel safe doing so.

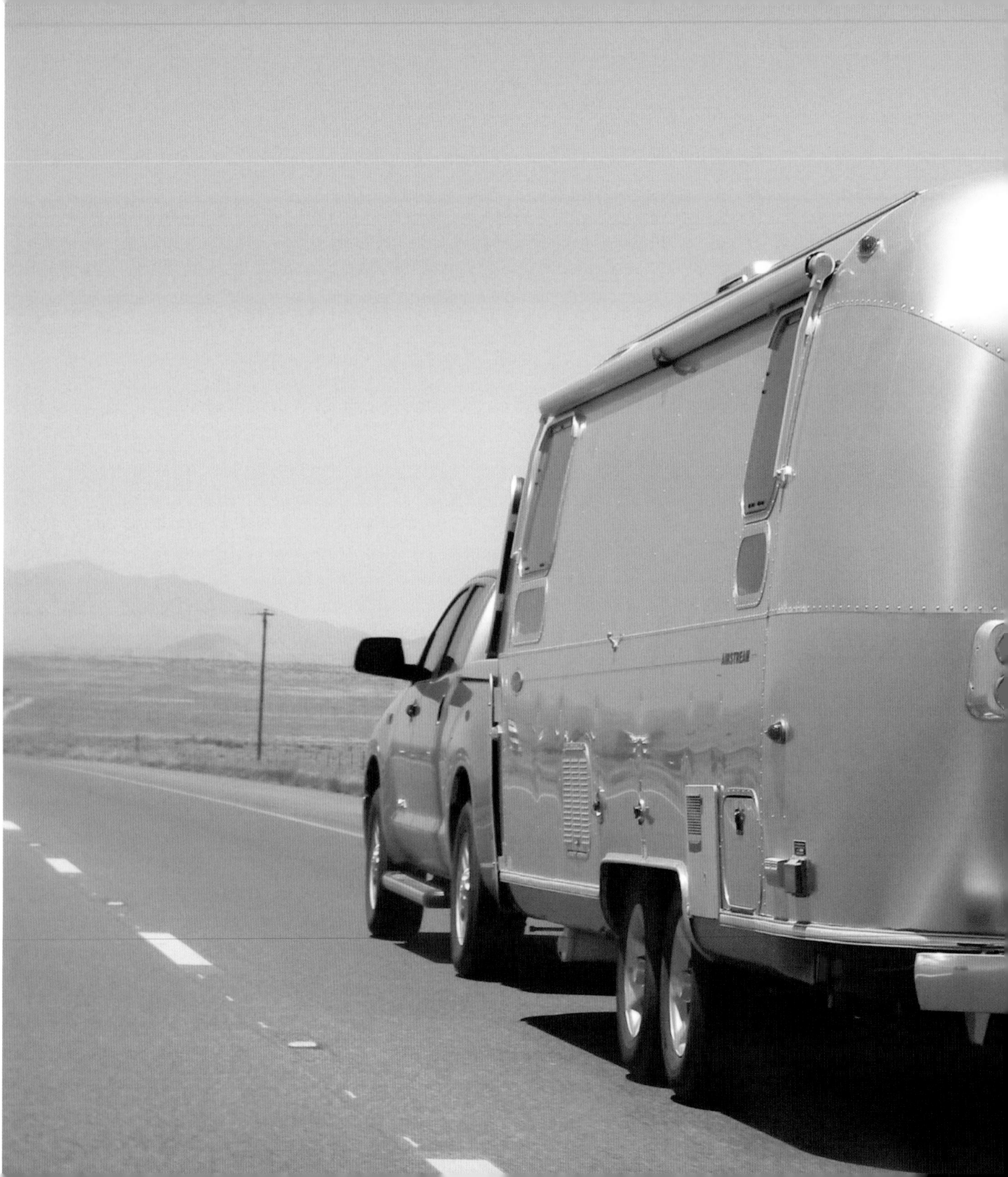

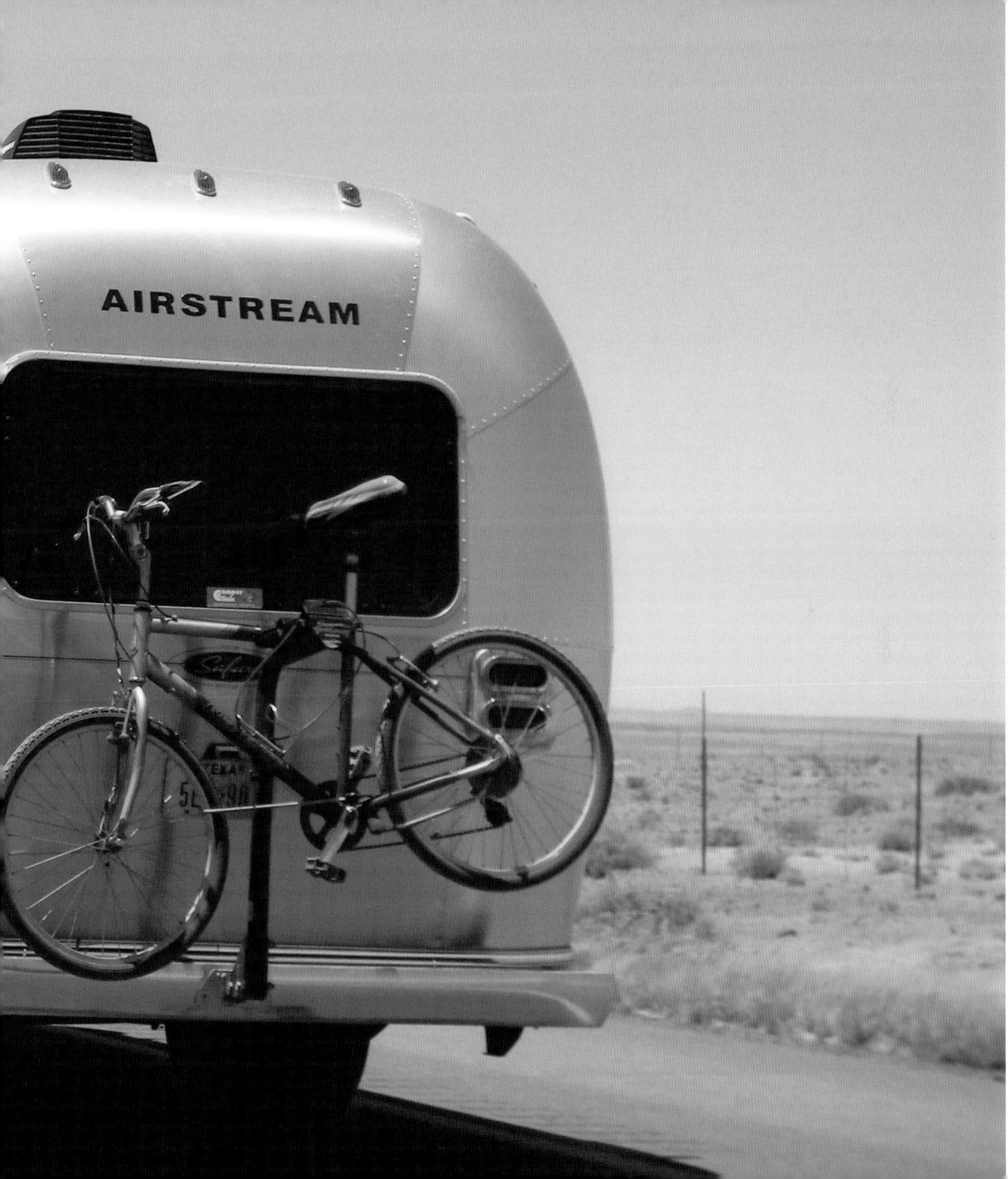
AIRSTREAM

(Left) Sign of the times — an abandoned old motel on a once thriving Route 66, now bypassed by the interstate highway.

(Above) Exploring small towns along the way is what makes a road trip memorable.

The road less travelled

In most countries, many state highways linking major cities have now been rebuilt to divert these routes around the small towns that used to make traffic slow down as it passed through them. This was because of the danger that the large load-bearing trucks, the main users of these major linking roads, caused to roads, pedestrians and other cars when they were asked to stop and start through the towns that developed alongside the old major road routes.

Nowadays these new wider, safer and straighter bypasses have cut many of these smaller towns right off, and what was once the main highway is now known as the 'old highway'. These new roads are built to cater for trucks travelling very long distances in a hurry to deliver loads, usually overnight, to major companies in the cities. They need roads that are safe, fast and as direct as the crow flies as possible; they don't care about ocean views or the world's biggest

Prairie Dog, scenic roads that wind through mountain passes or dramatic rock formations.

Most of those old roads were constructed and the towns built around them to cater for travellers who moved along at a much less rapid pace and who wanted to take time out to appreciate the natural wonders outside their vehicle. Most of us who travel in vintage caravans want that too, so I prefer to take the 'least use of freeways' option on the GPS to see what is over that hill, along that road or behind that lake. Sometimes I become lost and diverted way off my original route, and sometimes I become frustrated when I can't find my way back – but I often end up seeing something so spectacular that it all makes sense in the end. The moments spent during some of those unscheduled detours are often the best parts of the journey.

(Above) Be adventurous and don't be afraid to take the back roads sometimes.

(Left) Unplanned detours can sometimes be the best part of a journey.

(All) From beachfront sunrises to river sunsets...the view from your trailer can change as often as you want it to.

Check out the view

With a well-equipped trailer and a reliable car, the world is your oyster. There is some beautiful countryside out there in the world just waiting for you to discover it. The dramatic changes in scenery, the way the changing light casts a glow over the land at different times of the day, the excitement of the unknown as you drive towards a destination you've never been to before… All these things and more await you out there on the road.

If we want to stop all the good caravan parks from being turned into retirement villages full of cabins, we need to let the local authorities know how much we appreciate the great camping spots being there for us to use by using them. Camping in a caravan is a great way to explore places you've never been before and see things you never thought you'd see. It's time to take out that bucket list and start ticking off some places you've always wanted to go. Maybe this is driving across the old Route 66 in a classic car with a vintage camper in tow, maybe it's doing the traditional Aussie 'lap around the block', or taking the caravan across Europe, or to the Beach Hop in New Zealand.

Vintage caravans tend to make dreams come true and the allure of the road can be addictive. Most caravanners love to travel and have no hesitation driving thousands of miles to attend an event, visit a particular location or just for the sake of the road trip itself. Road tripping with a caravan is so much more fun than staying in hotels; you are free to roam wherever you want, but you've still got your very own bed to crawl into at the end of the day. It's home and away – it's the best of both worlds!

Once you've done it a few times, you will no doubt discover the joyful sensation of the wind in your hair as you drive with the windows down and the stereo turned up loud. You too will know how happy looking in the rear view mirror and seeing a window full of cheery bunting rolling along behind you makes you feel. Once you get a taste for the road tripping life, you'll be making plans to get out and about as much as you can to capture your own memories of what truly is a beautiful world.

CHAPTER 7
The on-site caravan

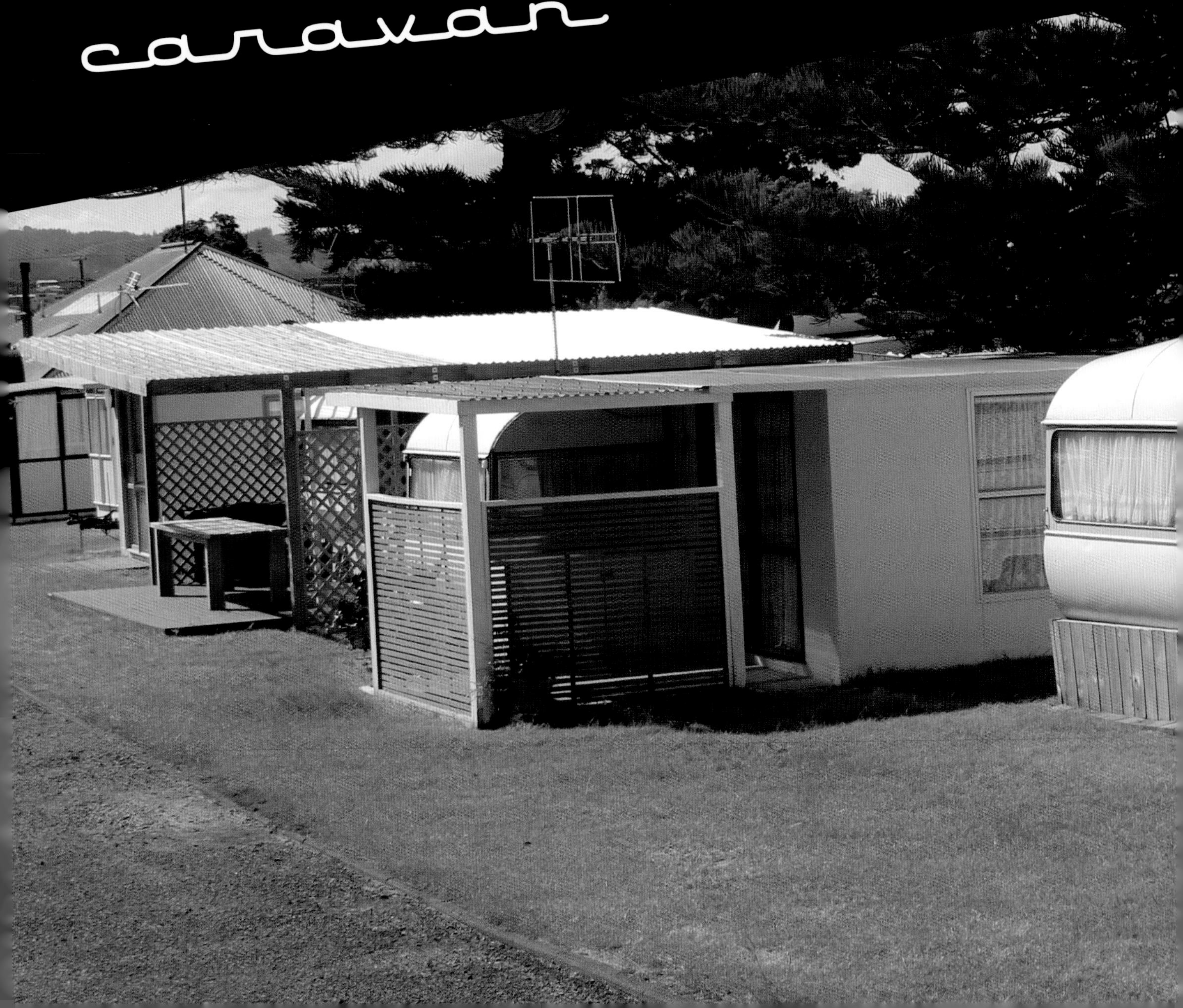

A place to enjoy

Not everyone who owns or restores a vintage trailer will want to take it out on the road. Many an old trailer has been converted specifically to use as an on-site space only. A lot cheaper to build than an entirely new room, a vintage trailer makes a fantastic spare room for guests, or for a teenager who needs his or her own space separate from the rest of the household.

So much better than just another room, vintage caravans are more like miniature homes, allowing for even greater privacy. Coming complete with a stocked wardrobe and pantry, running water, small kitchenettes and fridges, it is quite possible to remain housed up in a cozy caravan for days if need be. With everything you need close at hand, there's no better place to be than in your own miniature home.

(Left and above) An on-site trailer can become a great cubby house for grown-ups.

(Right) A beautifully decorated vintage trailer is highly conducive to creativity.

Become creative

Some older unused trailers that may never see the road again can still serve a useful life providing additional space outside the home for creative pursuits. Converted vintage trailers make the ideal studio for writers and artists and can be used as a dedicated crafting space for the crafters amongst us. I find a beautifully decorated vintage trailer is highly conducive to creativity, with much of my best writing work having been completed inside one.

I'm not sure why it is, but perhaps they remind us of the imaginative play in which we used to indulge as children, tucked away in our cubby houses or making forts far away from the grown-ups in the old garden shed down the back. Vintage vans are just the ideal places to make creative things happen: being inside a homely and thoughtfully decorated miniature house helps to create what feels like a time-free capsule where your worries melt away, allowing you to become completely caught up in the moment of creativity and inspiration.

A place to stay

A rusted old chassis and dodgy wheel bearings are not going to stop an old caravan from being used as a spare room. One of my favourite films of all time is *Harold and Maude* – I love the E-Type Jaguar, I love the theme of making the most of life, and I especially love that Maude lives in a converted old railway carriage. I remember watching that movie as a kid and thinking that I'd love to live in an old railway carriage, too; I think I loved the thought of running away on a train as much as I did my dream about gypsy caravans. Maybe that is why I love caravans so much – they are symbols of our ability to travel from one side of the country to the other, and there is some kind of juxtaposition in seeing a thing we usually associate with movement standing still.

When they do reach their own final resting places, caravans make good resting places for us to enjoy. Nothing is more inviting than an old vintage caravan sitting in a cottage garden, surrounded by flowers and garden gnomes, with a meandering path leading up to its door. All the tips and styling advice in this book can just as easily be applied to your non-travelling caravan, trailer, shed or garage, railway carriages or even an old bus. Indeed I can picture myself one day sitting on the deck of a big old Airstream with a spa pool in it, sipping Margaritas and watching the sunset over the rolling hills! I'll always have my 'hit the road' caravans but I've also lived permanently in one, which was the source of some of my happiest memories.

(Above right) Converted old railway carriages also make great getaway spaces.
(Right) When they reach their final resting places, caravans make good resting places for us to enjoy.

A place to escape

When the world and all its stresses become a bit overwhelming, we can often find ourselves just craving a bit of old-fashioned time out. Sometimes when things get really crazy and busy, I get this feeling that I want to just run away and escape it all somehow. I know that it's probably not always possible, but sometimes putting just a little bit of distance between ourselves and our problems can help to put things back into perspective.

Having a dedicated space outside the house or office where you can go and just sit, think, meditate or relax with a cup of tea or glass of wine is one of life's special treats, and certainly helps to ease an over-burdened mind. Converted trailers and caravans can provide you with that feeling of escape, even if they are never travelling anywhere again. They are restful, nap-inducing cocoons of tranquility.

You may well find, as I do, that you enjoy greater clarity of thought whenever you are inside your specially created small space. Times when the distractions of the world seem to be completely blocked out are when we find the time to listen to our mind's chatter and often clarify a situation or issue we have been grappling to resolve. Whenever you take time out to chill in a caravan you will find yourself smiling in no time.

Your neighbours may not understand your passion for the wreck of a caravan that arrives on your doorstep, but even the most ardent cynics will find it hard to resist the enchantment of a tastefully restored and decorated vintage caravan or trailer.

(Top left) Backyard trailers make ideal guest bedrooms.
(Centre left) If you don't own a vintage trailer you can hire one instead, such as this cutie at Enchanted Trails TV Park in Albuquerque, New Mexico, USA.
(Left) On-site caravan gardens are often filled with gnomes and flowers, sure to bring a smile to visitors' faces.

Beachside caravan parks such as this one in Piha, New Zealand, are fast becoming icons of a past era as they succumb to pressure from developers.

Trash or treasure?

It has been many years now since I lived in a trailer park, but I still have fond memories of my time spent there. When I first moved into a park as a permanent resident it wasn't long before the term 'trailer trash' became used around me – sometimes jokingly, sometimes not so much. There is an awful stigma that seems to accompany life in these low cost communities, which I hadn't truly understood until I had experienced it myself. If I could, I'd like to help dispel that stigma somehow.

Although unfortunate circumstances had brought me to this place in search of a cheap rental option, I ended up being so happy there that I chose to buy an on-site caravan when it came up for sale. I restored it and turned it into the girly heaven of a fairy princess, with pale yellow walls and white enamel trims inside the permanent annex, as well as full-length lace curtains across the windows. I gave away my old lounge furniture that was now too big for this small space and sat instead on purple velvet re-upholstered 1950s television chairs covered with silver star spangles, which I had sanded back, shellacked then sewn the fabric onto myself. Fairy lights adorned my windowsills and at the front of the sliding glass doors I created a flower-filled cottage garden complete with a picket fence and a wooden gate. Across the road from me was the laundry block, but I had my own ensuite with a washing machine connected at the back.

I was self-sufficient, the accommodation was affordable, I felt a lot less stressed because I didn't have to pay such a high rent, and everyone seemed accepting and friendly. I'd never known a sense of community like that before. So, I happily use the term 'trailer trash' to describe myself now, if it means that I once lived in a trailer park. Unlike the ignorance of those who perpetuate the stigma, I know the truth about living in close proximity to a group of people who have coped with some of life's more serious stresses. There was a camaraderie in our lowest moments that made us feel like our lot wasn't really so bad. There can be problems as with any community, whether it is online or in real life, with politics, gossip, power plays and the like. The lesson I learned in the trailer park was that small, close-knit communities learn to resolve their issues very quickly when they have to face each other the next day. Some residents of these trailer park communities can be struggling with the stresses of poverty as well, which can cause extra tensions, but there is also a shared understanding of the need for support during these times.

These days there is a noticeable increase in the number of people choosing, as I once did, to simply down-shift their lives and seek out lower cost living options. Paying ridiculously large mortgages for houses that far exceed our needs in size, and working excessive hours to pay for them, is not a dream; it sounds more like a nightmare! So often we don't make the time to take the

kids out on a camping adventure or a walk up a mountain. Then later in life especially, we want to get out and see some of this amazing stuff that the world has to offer beyond our immediate vicinity. Choosing a lower cost, permanent housing option allows for more freedom of movement to get out there and experience the world more, and hopefully even to work less.

Some permanent on-site trailers that I have seen during my travels are pretty flashy affairs, renovated and with immaculate front gardens. Always one to compliment a nicely kept garden, some residents I've spoken to said that they had lived in their trailers for 20 years or more. Imagine how much interest they have saved by not having a mortgage! That's not trashy, that's clever! Permanent on-site trailers, or caravans as they are called in caravan parks, can be styled, decorated and enjoyed as much as the ones on the road, whether they are in a trailer park or in a backyard. And the styling options using the space around a permanent trailer provides even greater scope for expression to bring it real street appeal. I love the quirkiness of some of these homes.

It is important to remember that these permanent trailers are homes for many people. I'd like it, if we could, to dispel any negative connotations of trailer park life and ease up on the associations of trailers with trash. For many people who live in them, choosing a trailer park life has brought them the existence of their dreams, and I think that is pure treasure!

(Left) A trailer park home can be a great option for many people who are choosing to 'downshift' their lives.

(Right) A caravan by the beach or a million dollar mortgage – which would you prefer?

(Left) Mimsy's Trailer Trash Tattoo studio is a 1960s Sunliner complete with a white picket fence and kitsch outdoor decorations.
(Right) The convenience of having a workplace on wheels makes a caravan a very appealing business option.

A place for business

Some older trailers are being bought up and renovated, never to be used as holiday accommodation ever again. Rather, they will be used for a wide range of business activities: coffee vending vans, antique stalls at vintage markets, ice cream stands at car shows, portable wedding photography backdrops, mobile stages and even tattoo studios. The possibilities for business ventures using vintage caravans are seemingly endless, with more and more springing up all the time. It is the convenience of having a workplace on wheels that makes a caravan a very appealing business option. For many enterprising individuals in the retail or food supply businesses, a converted vintage trailer is just right for creating a portable store that you can take home with you and re-stock at the end of the working day.

Although a full restoration or rebuild may be quite costly, a vintage van renovation will still cost a lot less than the ongoing costs associated with taking a lease on a piece of real estate, or building a purpose-built space. Older caravans are relatively cheap to come by in comparison to the bricks and mortar options and their portability opens up even greater marketing opportunities – have shop, can travel! Car shows are often good places to spot old vans hard at work. If you are considering using a vintage van for business, you will no doubt have noticed how many people seem to be drawn towards vintage caravans like magnets. This means that quite a few savvy businesses also use them as draw cards and conversation starters outside their place of business or as part of the business itself, with great results.

CHAPTER 8
The caravan community

A place to meet

You will find that owning a vintage caravan opens up your whole world, both geographically and socially. Even when I am out on the road travelling with my caravan alone, there is no shortage of friendly waves and comments wherever I go. Vintage vanners are generally a very sociable bunch.

Becoming involved in social groups that cater to vintage caravan or trailer owners is a great way to network with others, sharing tips and advice on restoration, trailer identification, information on forthcoming gatherings and rallies, or to organize weekends away. Many friendships are formed as a result of this common shared interest.

If you are new to the vintage caravan scene and shy about becoming involved, don't be. It doesn't matter what state of restoration or disrepair your caravan is in, or if you don't have a matching older car to go with it. Just get out there and try a few of the activities we discuss in this chapter to get you started, then watch the good times roll!

(All) After a few camping trips together, your new vintage vanner friends will seem more like family.

Car shows and hot rod events

My very first foray into the world of vintage vanning was at a car show. I was there to report on all the beautiful, shiny classic cars on display, but I found myself more drawn to the old caravans parked at the back. Hot rodders have enjoyed a great camaraderie over the years and many of them have created clubs and communities to share their knowledge with one another; quite a few of them also own an old caravan to tow behind their car.

Many hot rod and classic car clubs hold annual camp outs and weekend-long events that include fun activities such as observation runs, communal meals, trivia nights, music and dancing. In the past few years, as the increase in interest in older caravans has grown, a lot of these car show events are now incorporating vintage caravans into their open-to-the-public 'show 'n' shine' days. There is often camping available and plenty of opportunities to meet and mingle with other classic car and caravan lovers.

Many car shows now invite vintage caravans along to participate in their displays.

Attending open-to-the-public days is a great way to show off all the retro memorabilia you have collected in your caravan – just make sure you are prepared to talk to a lot of people who will no doubt want to reminisce with you about their early caravanning experiences. A board showing the make, model and build year of your trailer will help answer the most common enquiries you probably will get. The other question you will often hear is:

'Do you actually sleep in this?' I always laugh when I hear this one, as my caravan is often more of a home to me than my house, as I travel so much from show to show.

Car shows and rallies that welcome vintage caravans are often advertised in events guides in caravan and car magazines, but networking with other vintage trailerites is the best way to keep your ear to the ground on any upcoming events.

(All) A vintage caravan is the ultimate accessory for your hot rod, classic or custom car and has the added bonus of providing you with low cost accommodation at events.

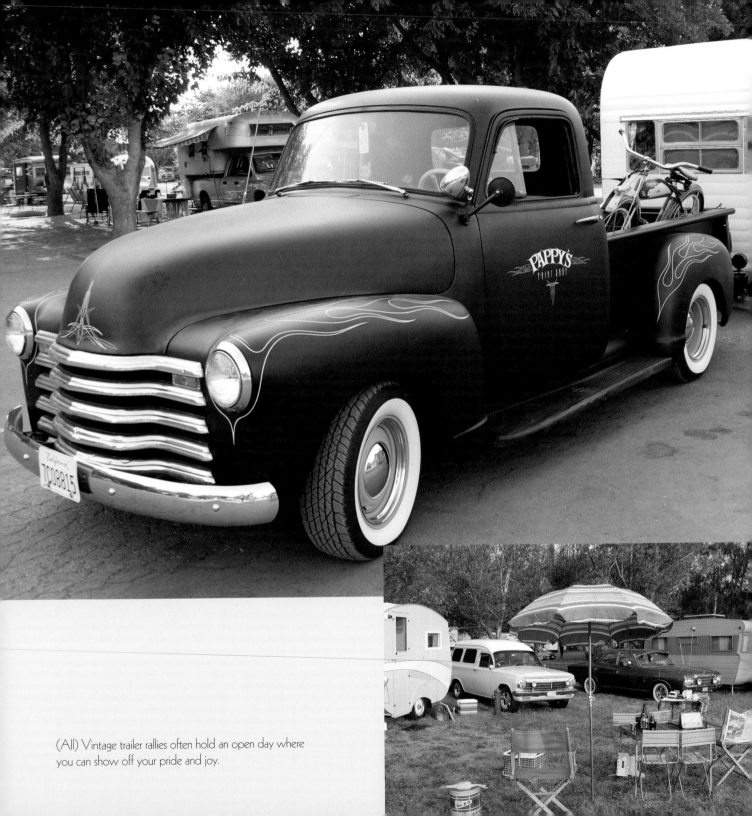

(All) Vintage trailer rallies often hold an open day where you can show off your pride and joy.

Trailer rallies

As well as organized car shows that may have a section for vintage trailers, most caravanning clubs and social groups now hold rallies for vintage trailers with hundreds turning up to many of these. Often held at a trailer park or show ground in a scenic destination, there is usually a good mix of people at these kinds of events, with some also catering for children and pets. These rallies are great fun and a wonderful way to get to know other vintage vanners in your local area; if you would like to participate with your own vintage trailer it pays to book up early, as some of the more popular rallies can be pre-booked for months in advance.

Trailer rallies usually last a whole weekend, with trailers starting to turn up on the Friday and leaving again on the Sunday. Sometimes there will be organized activities such as a pot luck dinner or bake off, workshops to attend, cruises to nearby points of interest, fancy dress nights and thrift store shopping sprees. If you would like to become involved in one of these types of events, make sure you contact the organizers as soon as you can to find out what the programme for that particular rally will be. It won't matter if your trailer hasn't been restored yet, as you will find everyone most welcoming to 'newbies'.

Social networking groups

These days the Internet has opened up a whole new way for us all to find one another. Online communities can be founded easily without going through all the legal red tape and paperwork, such as incorporation, that is required to establish a formal club. No matter what your interests are, there is sure to be a group out there in cyberspace that caters for exactly what you are into. A quick search on terms such as 'vintage trailer' or 'vintage caravan' will help you discover active interest groups nearest you. There are several online forums for vintage caravanners, many location specific; there are even make and model specific forums and social networking groups to join, where you can post photos and discuss the finer points of vintage van ownership.

Quite a few years ago, a couple of real-life sisters in the USA decided to start a small group of female friends to share their love for the great outdoors and activities such as fly fishing and horse riding – along with their love for their wildly decorated vintage trailers. They called their group Sisters on the Fly and adopted the motto 'We have more fun than anyone'. Now boasting several thousand members worldwide, this group has inspired many other such groups catering specifically for women campers. Many of these online groups organize regular get-togethers amongst themselves to quiet and beautiful locations, which provide members with the chance to meet other members and enjoy the best of what vintage caravanning is all about.

(Left) Fly fishing, horse riding, or just camping in their vintage trailers – Sisters on the Fly have more fun than anyone.

(Right) More and more women especially are finding themselves drawn to vintage caravanning.

(All) With a beautifully decorated trailer and a wardrobe in keeping with its era, camping can indeed be glamorous!

Glamping

'Glamping' is all the rage at the moment in the vintage vanning community. If you've never heard of it before, there is no doubt that you soon will! Created from the words 'glamorous' and 'camping', if you've never been the kind who likes to rough it in tents then a beautifully decorated vintage trailer could be your ticket to a whole new world where camping is certainly anything but rough.

The concept behind glamping is all about taking a little bit of luxury away with you, be it your best crystal wine glasses, your favourite satin pyjamas or your very best fine china tea sets. On a glamping adventure you really can have it all! Complete with touches of luxury such as chandeliers and pretty, girly decorative accessories, the glamper trailer has been transformed into a travelling haven of femininity for those who appreciate the finer things in life.

The concept of glamping has been made famous by several highly active groups such as Sisters on the Fly and the Loyal Order of the Glamper in the USA, but there are many more groups all around the world that cater to the growing number of people who like their camping with just a little touch of luxury added in. So, if you like the idea of getting outdoors, but prefer to take your 1,000-thread count sheets and down pillows with you, then glamping will be right up your alley!

Clubs

Unlike the wide variety of informal groups that have been created on the Internet and via social networking sites, established clubs generally have sets of rules and regulations pertaining to entry requirements, conduct and membership. They are also obliged to abide by legislation with regards to financial dealings and incorporation, such as appointing a committee, holding regular meetings, keeping strict financial records and taking minutes.

Although official caravan and trailer clubs have been around for almost as long as there have been caravans on the road and there are plenty that cater to owners of new caravans, there aren't yet a lot around for older caravans. Being in a club can help when it comes to things like getting group booking discounts at caravan parks, sourcing parts for your particular make or model of trailer and organizing events, and are ideal for networking with others with similar interests.

If there are no vintage caravan specific clubs in your local area, why not think about starting your own? Whether you create your own community of vintage caravanners or join an already established one, being around other people who share your passion will lead to a lifetime of friendships, adventure and new experiences that will have all your other friends scratching their heads.

It's OK, we understand and you are not alone, there are lots of us crazy caravan nuts out there all loving the adventure of life, and we'd love you to join us! See you out on the road!

(All) Joining a local vintage trailer club is a great way to link up and
network with others who share your passion.

About the author

Lisa Mora grew up enjoying what she describes as a gypsy lifestyle, travelling all around the world with her parents. She has lived in Australia, the USA, New Zealand, the Philippines, the Netherlands, Spain, Sweden, Greece and Sri Lanka, and up until she settled in the Sunshine Coast Hinterland of Australia six years ago, she had never lived in any one place for more than six months.

A change in circumstances in the year 2000 saw Lisa move into a small caravan in a caravan park. Having sold or given away most of her worldly possessions in order to fit into her new miniature home, Lisa took great delight in restoring and decorating this caravan to her heart's desire. Whilst living in the caravan park she came to the realization that she didn't need much to be happy; this period also allowed her time out from the world to pursue her writing dreams.

Lisa worked as a freelance writer specializing in event reviews before eventually being offered a job as a staff writer for a car magazine covering classic car shows and hot rod events. There she found herself more drawn towards the vintage caravans she would often see, and before long this interest developed into a passion she now describes as an 'obsession'. She went on to purchase several vintage caravans that she restored and eventually sold.

Knowing that there were plenty of others who shared her passion for vintage caravans, in 2011 Lisa created the world's very first *Vintage Caravan Magazine*, which now has several thousand subscribers all over the world. Lisa says that the gypsy urge still pulls her towards a life on the road and she still travels regularly, capturing the stories behind and images of vintage caravans and trailers everywhere she goes.

My first on-site caravan, which I renovated myself.

VINTAGE CARAVAN MAGAZINE

This is the first magazine in the world dedicated to vintage, classic and retro styled caravans and those who love them. Issued bi-monthly and showcasing caravans and trailers from across the globe along with restoration tips, interior styling ideas and event coverage, *Vintage Caravan Magazine* is a source of information and inspiration to all lovers of vintage caravans and trailers.
www.vintagecaravanmagazine.com

Index

Page references in bold refer to illustrations.

A DAVID & CHARLES BOOK
© F&W Media International, Ltd 2014

David & Charles is an imprint of F&W Media International, Ltd
Brunel House, Forde Close, Newton Abbot, TQ12 4PU, UK

F&W Media International, Ltd is a subsidiary of F+W Media, Inc
10151 Carver Road, Suite #200, Blue Ash, OH 45242, USA

Text © Lisa Mora 2014
Photographs © Lisa Mora except
Jason Bartley (NZ): 114 - 115, 128 (bl); Liz Cain (Aus): 147 (bl); Nicki Feltham
(UK) (www.nickifeltham.com): 54, 55, 101 (r), 109 (br); Ingrid Nelson (Myrtle &
Marjoram Photography) (USA): 62 (t); Sharon Sigmon (USA): 50 (tl); Monique
Weijers (NL): 51

A catalogue record for this book is available from the British Library.
ISBN-13: 978-1-4463-0451-8 paperback
ISBN-10: 1-4463-0451-5 paperback

ISBN-13: 978-1-4463-0452-5 paperback
ISBN-10: 1-4463-0452-3 paperback

Printed in China by RR Donnelley for:
F&W Media International, Ltd
Brunel House, Forde Close, Newton Abbot, TQ12 4PU, UK

10 9 8 7 6 5 4 3 2 1

Acquisitions Editor: Ame Verso
Desk Editor: Charlotte Andrew
Project Editor: Freya Dangerfield
Designer Manager: Sarah Clark
Production Controller: Kelly Smith

F+W Media publishes high quality books on a wide range of subjects.
For more great book ideas visit: www.stitchcraftcreate.co.uk

Important Notice: Disclaimer

The information presented in this book is intended for general guidance
only. Before towing a vehicle, you should always check the rules and
regulations applicable with your local transport authority. If disposing
of hazardous waste, please contact your local waste disposal authority
before you do so to ensure you fully comply with the law.

The author and publishers cannot be held responsible for any loss, harm
or damage to persons or property caused by the information contained
herein.